A BETTER STORY

BRANDON WILLIAMS

WESTBOW
PRESS®
A DIVISION OF THOMAS NELSON
& ZONDERVAN

WestBow Press books may be ordered through booksellers or by contacting:

WestBow Press
A Division of Thomas Nelson & Zondervan
1663 Liberty Drive
Bloomington, IN 47403
www.westbowpress.com
1 (866) 928-1240

ISBN: 978-1-5127-7954-7 (sc)
ISBN: 978-1-5127-7955-4 (hc)
ISBN: 978-1-5127-7953-0 (e)

Library of Congress Control Number: 2017904046

Print information available on the last page.

WestBow Press rev. date: 06/14/2017

CONTENTS

PREFACE

In the 1981 film *Raiders of the Lost Ark*, Indiana Jones, played by Harrison Ford, is hired by the US government to find the Ark of the Covenant before the Nazis do. The focal point of the movie and the adventure that ensues is finding the ark. Everyone's energy, time, money, and other resources are spent trying to find this one coveted item. The search captivated and consumed those seeking what had been lost.

In the same way, we, too, search for what has been lost. What we are seeking is not the ark of the covenant that, for the ancient Israelites, signified the presence of God. We seek what was lost when sin separated us from the presence of God. What did we lose? We lost contact with our image bearer who created us and gave us our identities. Since that time, we—meaning all of humanity—have been on a search to discover who we are (identity) and why we exist (purpose). We, like Indiana Jones and the others, spend all our energy, time, money, and other resources to define ourselves through work, recreation, social interaction, and religion. We long to know we are okay and that our being okay is not based on something shallow and temporal but on something significant, secure, and eternal.

This search for the ever-elusive feeling of being okay has brought me to the conclusion that our identities are scrambled and confused by thousands of influences in the world around us and only reordered and redefined when they are solidly established within God's Word. It has also brought me to the conclusion that identity is not *an* issue for people. It is *the* issue that must be resolved if we are to live in the fullness of joy that is possible in Christ. Coming to a secure identity in Christ is not a cure-all, but it is necessary to resolve our internal identity conflict if we wish to be whole.

If we are to overcome our identity struggles, it will require a twofold approach. On the one hand, we must identify and deal with the confusion dealt to our identities by all the influences from our past and present. We must discern what they have taught us about ourselves and life and separate what is true and what is fiction. However, to only seek to understand why we are the way we are and what has made us this way is to fall short of a resolution to our crises. More is needed. Honestly, this is where secular psychology and most books written about our identities in Christ fall short.

If we stop at recognizing the false truth (Can there be such a thing?) that we've been taught through our experiences, we've only won half the battle. The other half is won by establishing a legitimate truth in our lives. Once we've recognized the holes in our identities, we need something—or someone—to fill in the gaps. This is where God's Word comes in. When we overlay God's Word onto what we have learned through experience and the influences in our lives, we are able to see clearly what is fact and what is fiction.

To say we know the cause (the experiences and influences that made us the way we are) or we know the answer (the truth that God's Word teaches us) is to know only part of the equation. To solve the problem, we must combine the two. It would look something like this:

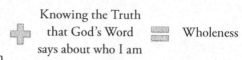

Understanding the experiences & influences that have made me the way I am ✚ Knowing the Truth that God's Word says about who I am ▤ Wholeness

This book aims to help you complete this equation. First, we discover the experiences and influences that shaped us to see ourselves and life the way we do. Then we apply God's Word to our lives so that we are able to separate fact from fiction and establish a firm identity we can truly build our lives upon.

This book is written for anyone who has ever struggled with condemnation, feelings of unworthiness, or the performance trap of only feeling loved and accepted when you live up to your, or someone else's, expectations. If you not only read this book but also apply the principles that are taught, I truly believe you will experience the words of Jesus in John 8:32: "Then you will know the truth, and the truth will set you free." (Except where noted, all scriptural references are to the NIV edition of the Bible.)

ACKNOWLEDGMENTS

To the staff at Connection Church—there's no other group of people I'd rather be on this journey with than all of you.

To Joey Fennell, Shawn Corbett, Chad Wiggins, and Cynthia Lee who have been armor bearers and a great help in this journey toward discovering my identity in Christ: thank you for standing with me through the struggles.

To Dr. John Walker—without you this book would not have been written. First of all, I would not be here to write this book if it were not for your heart for the hurting. Second, it is your genius that I have attempted to relay to others through this writing. The lessons I learned from you while at the Blessing Ranch have forever changed my life and, in turn, the lives of those God has called me to minister to.

To my mother and father—thank you for always pushing me to be my best, for always giving me unconditional love, and for always being there to listen and give advice.

To my three boys—Dake, Jackson, and Reid—my greatest desire for your lives is that you discover and live in your identities in Christ. If that is all I accomplish in this lifetime, my life will be an overwhelming success.

Finally, to my wife, Susan, there aren't enough words to say all that you have meant to me in my life. You stood with me through the good days and the bad. You've been my biggest supporter and the one who has always reminded me of my calling and the power of God to keep going. Thank you. "Take my hand, I'll help you stand, and we will walk together" (source unknown).

INTRODUCTION

My Story

I moved to the small town of Statesboro, Georgia, in 1985, at the age of ten. Statesboro is still a small town, but it was much smaller back then. It was the kind of town in which everyone knew each other, and your identity was largely connected to who your family was. A question I got quite often back then was, "Hey, boy, who do you belong to?" Of course, this was a way of asking, "Who are your parents, and are you from here?" I finally just started answering the question with the simple statement, "I'm not from around here." This answer brought raised eyebrows on more than one occasion.

I struggled to find my identity in Statesboro for several years. Since no one seemed to like me the way I was, I decided I would re-create myself into someone different. I can still remember one spring afternoon, standing on the playground of my elementary school, and seeing a pretty blonde-haired girl walking across the football field. The thought that popped into my head was, *I'd like to have one of those one day.* So the next several years of my life were spent becoming the type of person I thought a girl like that would want. I tried to wear the right clothes, say the right things, and hang out with the right people. I worked hard at athletics because I figured that was one way I could find the popularity I hoped to attain. Lo and behold, it actually worked! After my best attempt at a "re-creation,"

I finally met my childhood sweetheart, who eventually became my wife. However, it would be many years later that I would begin to grow into the identity that God truly intended for me.

The sad part is that many of us never outgrow these adolescent attempts at defining or re-creating ourselves through appearance and "stuff." Many of us are still searching for the illusive security that only comes from an identity grounded in Jesus Christ.

Identity is who we are. It is what we are known as and what we are known for. It is basically a description of our existence. It's not limited to what others think about us. It is, maybe even more so, what we think of ourselves.

Everyone has aspects of their identities that they would like to change. Many of us would like a fresh start or even a completely new beginning. We have all had experiences we wish would not have happened or would have happened differently. These experiences are powerful and have shaped how we define ourselves. In many cases, these experiences have given us a false identity or an untrue understanding of who we are.

Our experiences often lie to us about our identities. In order to know who we are, we must be able to refute these lies. I have come to believe that much of modern counseling and psychology falls short of allowing us to be truly free. It seems to identify our problem without offering hope for a solution. It would be like having the flu and only treating the cough. Unless we have something to stand upon, it is logical to conclude that we simply cannot stand. We may be able to recognize the problem of a false identity, but until we have something powerful enough to overcome it, we do not have any hope of escaping its hold on us.

The Gospel Story

The truth is that we are all sinners. We have all rebelled against God and committed wrong acts against Him. Because of this, we—humanity—have fallen under God's judgment and are rightfully condemned. The good news is that God loved us so much that He made a way for us to be made right with Him. He did this by sending Jesus to take the judgment we deserved. When we come to faith in Jesus as our Lord and Savior, we trade our wretchedness for His righteousness. We are given the perfection that only Jesus has ever attained. It's important to remember that this is something that we cannot do on our own and must simply receive from God. It is not based on our performances but on Jesus's work on the cross.

The problem for many people is that they never "do right" long enough to feel they can come to God. We have to realize the Christian life is not a "bargain." We aren't working a deal with God. It's all God! We didn't decide to let God forgive us; He chose to forgive us through Jesus. If God forgiving us was based on our decisions, we could somehow decide we don't deserve it and nullify the agreement. But our salvation doesn't work that way. God chose to save us through His Son. It's not based on what we did or what we would do but on what He has done through Jesus.

It's interesting that Satan is the prince of this world, and the world's system is based on performance. It's not coincidental that God's system is based not on what we do but on whose we are. They are polar opposites. Yet Satan's greatest weapon is manipulating us to transpose his system onto God's system. It can be terribly confusing and leads us to an identity crisis with God and ourselves. Many people today are still working to attain what can only be received from Jesus.

When we, by faith, make this transfer of wretchedness for righteousness, the Bible tells us we are no longer under condemnation. It also tells us that we are made a "new creation" as we are given a new identity, a new heart (center of our being), and filled with the very presence of God. Did you catch that? What we have been working so hard for—a new identity and a re-creation of ourselves—is freely given through faith in Jesus. It is in this relationship, and this relationship only, that we will ever be secure in our identities.

I want you to understand this transfer of wretchedness for righteousness because it is the key to a better story in your life. In fact, this transfer is known as the gospel story. This book is about how our better story is found in the gospel story. What we are going to discover is that our better story is really not even about us at all. It is all about God's glory, not ours. It is His story, not mine.

Your Story

I wrote this book because I truly believe God has a better story for your life. I believe there is more that God wants for you and a freedom you have yet to experience. I believe God wants to take the pen from your hand and write what can only be written with a life that is surrendered to Him.

I want to be clear that God writing your story doesn't mean it will not be full of challenges, trials, and difficult days. God never promised us a trouble-free world. In fact, He told us just the opposite when Jesus said, "In this world you will have trouble. But take heart! I have overcome the world" (John 16:33). Even as God has begun to write a better story in my life, I still have tough days and obstacles that seem like mountains. In this book I share a lot of my story. I share many of the challenges and disappointments with you. I want you to understand my circumstances haven't changed. I did. God transformed my heart and is now transforming my mind. I have finally learned what it is to live in the freedom that comes from Jesus and the truth of His Word.

This book is primarily written from the view of someone who is "in Christ." However, I believe it will also be beneficial to non-Christians as they see the power of a relationship with Jesus.

Whether you are a longtime follower of Christ or simply curious, God wants to write His story with your life. A story that brings Him glory and you the fulfilment you've been looking for. Let's get started on our journey toward giving God the pen and letting Him write a better story with our lives.

CHAPTER 1

❖

THE RERUN

We all had one. Some of us still have one. Many of us gave up on ours a long time ago. Some of us are jealous that others still have one. Some of us have been embittered by their illusiveness. We often mock those who pursue theirs.

What am I referring to? Dreams. Just admit it. When you were a child, there was something you wanted to be. There was something in you that said you were destined for greatness. There was a reason for your existence. It was a dream. It was big—really big. It was much bigger than you were. It was big enough to impact the world.

I'm no different. I had a dream as a child. My dream centered on a ball made of horsehide, wrapped around yarn, wound tightly on a rubber core, and held together by 108 red stitches. Well, obviously that's just an elaborate way to say I wanted to be a major league baseball player. In fact, that's *all* I wanted to be. If you asked me when I was ten years old what I was going to major in at college, I would have told you baseball. When you told me there was no major for baseball, I would have confidently and defiantly told you, "Then I'm not going."

Baseball was life! It's all I ever wanted to do. It was the one thing that motivated me in school because I couldn't play if I didn't keep good grades. I loved it, and in a strange way, it seemed to love me back. Baseball was how I was known. It was where I found my identity. It supported my ego and was a refuge when nothing else seemed to be right with the world. Not to mention, I was pretty good at it. Or so I thought.

I experienced a lot of success in the game through Little League and into my high school years. I had enough success, in fact, to earn a very small scholarship to Georgia Southern University, a well-respected Division I college program in my hometown of Statesboro. Looking back, that's where my dream began to die.

At Georgia Southern, I went from being the proverbial big fish in a small bowl to a small fish in a huge bowl. For the next two years, I struggled and amassed a whopping three at-bats during that time. I continued to work hard even though my dream was on life support, and the plug could have been pulled at any time. It felt like I was stuck in the rerun of a bad movie every day of my life.

My life seemed to be one failure after another. Every day was a reminder that I didn't measure up to the other players. Each practice or game that I watched reinforced the fact that I simply wasn't good enough. With each passing day, I inched closer to the death of my dream as my failures, shortcomings, and inadequacies were relived and then replayed time and time again in my mind.

Things began to change between the second and third year of my college career, and I made some good strides. I actually improved a lot through the fall and early spring practices, and heading into the season, it seemed I would have a good chance to play and possibly even start in several games.

Once the season started, I realized our coaching staff didn't think as highly of my improvements as I did. Let's just say I really didn't see the field a lot. This led me to have a conversation with our head coach. (We'll refer to him as Skip, since that's what we called him.)

Looking back now, the conversation is humorous. In the moment, not so much. Our talk took place one spring afternoon as we were leaving practice, and it went something like this.

Skip, can I talk to you for a second?

Yeah, big guy. (He called us all big guy. Honestly, I'm still not sure he knew my name!)

Well, Skip, I was wondering what else I need to do to get in the lineup more. I feel I've played pretty well when I've gotten a chance, but I'm not getting much opportunity.

(Then came the nail in the coffin of my dream.)

Well, big guy, I think you are overestimating your talent and ability.

That was it.

Really? End of conversation? Hit the showers? See you tomorrow? Or you're not good enough to even bother me with silly questions?

It was at this moment that I realized it was over. I finished out the season and then hung up my spikes forever. Dream over. Gone.

I still highly respect my former coach. He was one of the best to ever coach the game at the college level. To be honest, he could have been dead-on accurate about my ability. Either way, that conversation

3

brought an end to my dream and a separation from the god I served for nearly twenty-one years.

College baseball is the only thing I've ever quit. Well, unless you include drinking, chewing tobacco, cussing (for the most part), and gambling. Oh yeah, I also pretty much quit golf. After giving up the aforementioned vices, I found that golf wasn't much fun!

Baseball was the only thing I ever quit, and I don't think it's coincidence that I have two recurring dreams. One is that I can't get to church on time and don't have my notes for the sermon. I'm sure there are people more spiritual than I who can dissect that dream and tell me what I'm really feeling. I've just determined that I'm afraid I'll be late and unprepared for church. If there's a deeper, more-horrifying meaning, please let me live in ignorance.

The other recurring dream is that I return for my last two years of eligibility at GSU and complete my baseball career. It's as if my college baseball experience is still being replayed through my head almost twenty years later. I simply can't seem to escape it.

I imagine you can relate to my experience in some way. It may not be athletics, but some other area of your life seems to haunt you. It's that person, place, or thing in life that just won't leave you alone. Like an old episode of a sixties sitcom, it just seems to continually replay itself.

For some of us, the rerun is more like a horror story. For others, the rerun resembles the can't-miss blockbuster movie that, no matter how many times you watch it, always seems to end, leaving you unsatisfied. Some of us would label it that one thing that, if we could just get over it, our lives would be exponentially better.

Truthfully, we all have "it." Some of us may have more than one of it. While it may be different for each of us, the effects are the same. To think we can somehow escape its grasp seems to be overestimating our abilities.

If this is true for you, I bet I can almost tell you the pattern of your life. You, like most people, want to be a good person. You want to represent Christ in the things you do. Your days are spent trying to hold up your end of the bargain and do things the right way. That's admirable. But how's that working for you?

Most likely, you do well until you trip, stumble, or fall and drop your end of the deal. When you stumble, you're flooded with guilt that turns into condemnation. As you struggle under the weight of condemnation, a burden too heavy for anyone to live under, much less thrive under, you find yourself in a familiar place: burned out and exhausted from bargain-based living. In our Christianese language, we call this legalism.

This funk lasts for days, weeks, months, or even years until you "do right" long enough to settle your conscience and gain enough courage to slip back into God's presence. Once again, we put our noses to the grindstone and try to be God's good little boys or good little girls. We audition for God's love and perform for Him like a dancing chicken at the county fair.

It works for a while. But then we sense that our performances are no longer worthy of God. We finally trip, stumble, and fall again. And once again, we feel the deep shame and guilt of having let God and others down with our poor performances. Sound like you?

Let's look at another scenario. Your life is moving merrily along. Things seem to be clicking. You're solid in your marriage or singleness. You're productive and would even categorize yourself as having at least an average amount of self-esteem. You feel like you have a purpose in life and can actually make a difference in the world and in God's kingdom. If you were to rank your life from one to ten, with ten being the best, it would fall between seven and ten. Overall, things are good.

Then it happens. You see "them." They call. You're reminded of "it," and everything falls apart. The quality of your life goes from seven to ten to one to three. Shame and guilt for past failures or hurts flood your mind, and you feel as though your face is flushed, either from a loss of blood or from all of the blood in your body rushing to your head. At this point, you're sure everyone around you recognizes what just happened because, in your mind, it's impossible to hide what you feel inside.

You hate yourself for feeling this way and for letting them or it have so much control over your life. Condemnation now overwhelms you, not only for what you did with them or it or what they did to you, but also for the way those events still control your life.

You live at this low level until you finally bury the encounter with them or it. You numb the pain by finding an exit through busyness, distractions, alcohol, drugs, pornography, sex, food, sleep, or just giving up and quitting. The list could go on forever.

Finally, after a lot of time, you pull yourself up by your bootstraps to give it another go. But in the back of your mind, you know this next act in the story of your life will end with disappointment, guilt, and condemnation—the same way countless others have—when your fall from grace is once again triggered by them or it.

Maybe this one fits you: You're a driven person. Life clicks for you when you're "getting it done." You like to build things like your company, your church, other people, your community, or your reputation and influence. You like to see progress. First, there's nothing wrong with those qualities. In fact, we need people with these qualities, and in many ways, they are very admirable. If we all had the mindset that there's no reason to push things forward, then nothing of significance would ever be accomplished. Someone has to be the sparkplug, the visionary, and the one willing to push the flywheel.

The problem for this type of person comes when things aren't getting done. Things aren't being built, and progress isn't being made. The company isn't growing. People aren't listening. The community isn't changing, and it all seems to be a reflection on your reputation and dwindling influence.

You start to feel a sense of panic. This feeling could result from what you perceive as your failures through the events of one day or a lifetime of blood, sweat, and tears. Regardless of the amount of time involved, everything within you wants to scramble to hold on to what seems to be slipping away. Yet the tighter you try to hold on, the more you seem to choke the life out of it.

The fear that grips you at the thought of losing what you've tried to build is bad enough, but it does not compare to the fear that paralyzes you when you think someone could pass you or accomplish more than you. You are riveted by envy of those who seem to be getting it done at a greater level than you. You even find yourself looking for opportunities to slander those who might get ahead of you. When you hear that something didn't go their way, you pretend remorse on the outside. But on the inside, there is a part of you that is smiling, even if it is suppressed in the dark corners of your heart. To say you are competitive would be an understatement. It is your value and worth that are on the line, not just a win or loss. A win means acceptance with God and others. A loss means condemnation on all fronts, especially in your own heart.

How about this one? Does it sound like you? You've never felt really secure in who you are. You were never the popular one in school. You might not describe yourself as disliked but probably just not noticed. At least not noticed to the level you would have liked to be or by the people you desired to have take notice of you. You do well until you see someone—either in person, a magazine, or on television—that represents everything you feel you aren't. You begin to feel a churning in your stomach and jealousy in your heart. You think, *Why should they have it all?*

There's probably a specific quality or attribute that bothers you the most. Is it wealth? Charm? Personality? Charisma? Material possessions? Courage? How about beauty? Think about this. If a girl is jealous of another girl because of her beauty, she does not hate her because she is beautiful but because she concludes that beauty gives the other girl greater value and worth.

Now think about it on the flip side. The girl with the beauty becomes obsessed with her beauty. To lose her beauty would be to lose her value and worth. Her beauty becomes an idol because it consumes her to the point that staying beautiful drives her life.

One girl is fighting to *attain* her value and worth. The other girl is fighting to *maintain* her value and worth. Both are miserable. It's exhausting just to think about it! It's an extremely exhausting cycle to live in.

Regardless of which of these scenarios you identify with, the shared outcome is condemnation. Condemnation unleashes its brute force in an all-out attack on our identities. The destructive force of condemnation is seen most clearly in our view of ourselves and ultimately in our relationships with God and other people. Our thought process goes something like this: *I know I'm not okay. I can't accept me. There's no way God or anyone else will either.*

In marriage, our condemnation causes us to lash out at our spouses, spewing discord and even hate in our verbal and nonverbal communications. We withdraw from conversation and physical contact, and begin to live under the same roof while living separated. Behind our behavior is the question, "How could someone truly love me like this?"

Fear, doubt, and even paranoia begin to creep into your mind and eventually settle into your heart. You even begin to create scenarios in your head of what the other person is doing. Thoughts of marital unfaithfulness begin to run wild through your mind. You begin to connect dots that may or may not exist to form a picture that is inconsistent with reality. Finally, all that is built up inside you must come out, and it doesn't come out gently. One's relationship with his or her spouse is drastically affected by the power of condemnation.

The question, "How could someone truly love me like this?" is not limited to marriages. This same line of thought touches every relationship. Again, if I know in my heart that I'm not okay, surely everyone else knows and will find it impossible to truly love me.

Our hearts are filled with the disappointment, pain, and shame that, when combined, make up the hurt that is the undeniable work of condemnation. The truth is we reflect our wounded hearts onto the hearts and lives of others. As we do this, we endure another barrage of condemnation and accusation as the enemy within tries to pick us apart. The cycle of condemnation seems to always find us, while the fullness of life seems to always pass us by.

The apostle Paul made a bold statement in Romans 8:1, declaring, "there is now no condemnation for those who are in Christ Jesus." Basically, because Jesus took our sin upon Himself and took the punishment of God's wrath on the cross, sin was condemned once and for all in Christ for those who trust in Him. Yet, even with that great news being talked about so much in Christian circles, Christians are more prone to live in condemnation than anyone else I see.

The good news of Jesus is that we no longer have to hide in our shame and guilt. We can come boldly before God's throne to receive grace and mercy. There is no bargain to be made. There is no legal requirement to be fulfilled. There is only faith in the finished work of the cross.

Contrary to much that has been taught in our churches, condemnation does not serve our relationship with God well. God does not love us more because we feel guilty, and our guilt does not pull us to God; it pushes us away. Humanity has always responded to condemnation and guilt by running from God, not to Him. Our original parents, Adam and Eve, did the same thing. When they realized they had sinned, they actually tried to hide from God. That's the worst game of hide-and-seek you could ever play!

When we allow condemnation to separate us from God, we have constructed an imaginary boundary between Him and us. We are missing out on a relationship with the Creator of the universe because of a barrier that was destroyed by Jesus and only exists in our minds and hearts. It sounds awfully stupid when you think of it that way.

Whether you find yourself in one or more of these scenarios, it won't take long before you grow weary and begin to ask questions like these:

> Will I ever get beyond this?

> Can I get beyond this?

Does God just want me to be like this?

Why have I prayed so much, yet this will not go away?

Can I possibly be a Christian and still feel this way?

Is this just "the way I am"? Is this my true identity?

Then, for many, the questions turn into a definitive statement that says, "I will never get beyond this!" This seems a far cry from the abundant life Jesus promised in John 10:10, doesn't it?

What are we to do? How do we access the abundant life of Christ? How do we live life full of the fruit of the Spirit and free from condemnation? My prayer is that throughout the rest of this book, we discover God's plan for delivering us from the chains of condemnation and into our true identities in Christ.

I want to encourage you to do three things.

1. You need to commit to be persistent. This includes the materials we explore together as well as faithfully utilizing the tools you will receive for the rest of your life.
2. You need to commit to participate. Don't just read to complete the book. Participate in it. Explore your heart. Do the exercises. Be honest with yourself and with God. If you read this book so you can check it off your list, you will miss the point and the blessing!
3. You need to commit to stick it out. Sometimes healing is painful, and sometimes things seem to get worse before they get better. Stick with it, knowing that God is working in you through the principles He's given us and the power of His Word.

I want to emphasize that none of the scenarios, or any you could add to my list, should dominate any follower of Christ. The quality of our lives should be high. It is God's promise. I didn't say that the circumstances of our lives would be perfect. Nor did I say that trials and difficult days do not lie ahead of us. What I am saying is that our lives should be full of love and joy, peace and patience, kindness and goodness, faithfulness, gentleness, and self-control (Galatians 5:22, 23). These are the attributes of God, given by God, not the attributes of humankind produced by humankind.

CHAPTER 2

SORE SPOTS

In chapter 1, I spoke of a couple of dreams that I have from time to time. There is another dream I've had, but probably not quite regularly enough to refer to it as "recurring." In this strange dream, I end up in a public place, wearing nothing but my underwear! Please tell me you've had it, too, and I'm not completely insane. Okay, I can feel myself slipping into condemnation. Just kidding ... Sort of.

I don't know why I have occasionally dreamed I went to Walmart, the grocery store, or even church in my underwear. (Again, if you know some horrifying reason that I have had this dream, just keep it to yourself.) I just assume it has been during times I felt especially anxious and vulnerable. The most distressing part of the "underwear dream" is being, for the most part, naked in front of large groups of people. There is something intimidating and horrifying about that type of vulnerability.

That's kind of how I feel right now. Not because I'm writing this in my underwear; that's a mental picture no one should be made to endure. But I feel vulnerable and "naked" because I want to share my personal scenario with you. I've already shared a few scenarios that we find ourselves in, but if you'll indulge me for a bit, I'm going to share mine with you in hopes that, in the end, it will be a source of encouragement to you.

As I look at the scenarios described in the first chapter, I can honestly say I do not fit any one of them. I fit *all* of them! The reason I was able to describe them is because I have lived them. Okay, I've never been a girl who was envious of another girl's beauty, but you could substitute dozens of other insecurities in the place of beauty and describe my struggle to attain or maintain value and worth through my performance.

I have been blessed to pastor what I believe to be the greatest church on the face of the planet, Connection Church in Statesboro, Georgia (obviously, I'm a little biased). We have seen God do so many amazing things over the last several years. Sometimes I have to step back and ask myself, "Is this really happening?" We have seen hundreds of salvations and baptisms, people finding authentic community with other believers, in addition to God developing a heart to serve others in people who were once only self-serving and entitled.

I'm not telling you these things to pat myself on the back. I'm telling you the things God has done because I want you to understand that for the first four and one-half years, I wasn't able to enjoy any of it. Looking back, I realize I had a couple of sore spots that seemed to constantly nag me. Sore spots are those things that, when poked, cause us to spiral into condemnation and despair.

For me, sore spot number one dealt with me not being good enough because of things in my past. I grew up as an only child and felt the weight of high expectations from an early age. High expectations are not bad things. I learned from my college baseball days that the reason people don't have high expectations of you is because they don't think you have very much to offer. So in no way do I blame my parents for the feelings of those pressures. While people in our lives may specifically impose those pressures on us, they are generally a part of our experiences because we live in a world built on a system of performance.

The problem wasn't the pressures I, or anyone else who's ever existed, felt and lived with. The problem was the false identity the pressures created. The world tells us that if we perform well, we will be loved and valued. If we don't perform well, we will not be loved and valued. It basically says, "Only the best have value." But we know that superiority doesn't bring security because those who we view as superior still have the same, or more, struggles than we do.

Sore spot number two dealt with me not being good enough because of the unknowns of the future, especially regarding the church. I was haunted by the question, "Would we win?" I even developed number goals with our leadership team in the first month of the church because I wanted to see if people thought we could make a significant difference. I also had to quantify everything, so I could know when we won. It was, of course, shrouded beneath a false façade of needing to clarify our vision. Nothing is wrong with developing goals and identifying the "win" for your organization. You must do this. The problem is when attaining the goals and winning determine our significance. As I stated in the first chapter, a win for you means acceptance and worth, while losing means condemnation and a loss of value.

I lived in fear of losing. Losing to me was not having the fastest-growing ministry in our area. Losing was when a family visited and never came back. It was a message that didn't go like I wanted it to go. It was a negative comment that may or may not have been rooted in reality. Fear gripped me every time I saw another pastor's post on Twitter or Facebook because it poked my sore spot of insecurity and made me ask, "Do people like them more than me?" and, "Will people follow them more than me?" The real question stirring in my heart was, "Do they have more value than me?" It was to the point that I couldn't be on social media at all.

My sore spot was poked anytime a new church started. I wanted to be kingdom-minded and rebuked the competitiveness. But nothing could keep the thoughts from coming back time and time again. In my heart, I wanted to wish them well. I even asked some to partner with us, even if it meant me not being the senior pastor. Even today, I have to sort through which of my actions were driven by a desire to see the kingdom grow and which were driven by the fear of being left behind and no longer valued. The fear that they would pass us or be more effective than us kept me up at night and wore the lining in my stomach thin.

What do these sore spots have in common? They all exist because of a false identity. A false identity develops and becomes true to us, but in reality, it is not true at all. A false identity tells us that our values are wrapped up in our performances and not in whose or who we are. My identity struggle became a huge source of condemnation that constantly pounded at my mind and my soul. These sore spots seemed more like inescapable traps. I felt trapped. And there did not seem to be any real grounds to have hope.

You need to understand Satan's goal in condemnation is not to hinder but to ultimately destroy us. I know this is true because in March of 2013, I was on the brink of destruction. I had experienced lows before, but not this bad. Over the years, my highs got lower and shorter, and my lows got longer and deeper. It got so bad that I didn't even work the last two workdays leading up to our Easter service. What preacher doesn't work half of Easter week? Even though I knew over a thousand people would be in attendance to celebrate our risen Savior, I couldn't stand the thought of going to the office or preparing another message. I was in a deeper pit than I had ever been in. I truly did not believe I would ever escape.

With escape from my mental, emotional, and spiritual prison seeming impossible, I began to try and think of other ways to escape. Talking to people about the reruns became part of the rerun, and I no longer had any interest in the futility of conversation. I thought of quitting the ministry. In fact, I wished that somehow I would just be asked to quit. That would be an exit.

I wish I could say I didn't think of quitting on life in an irreversible and final way. In my sick state, I thought, *Maybe it would be simpler, even better, to exit this prison and my pain once and for all.* It makes me sick to my stomach to write those words. I have to fight a feeling of condemnation for having thought them. But even in such a blinded state, I could see the selfishness and cowardice of that action and couldn't bear the thought of leaving my wife and children to fend for themselves.

Several months earlier, my wife and I attended a pastor care conference at Newspring Church in Anderson, South Carolina. I had heard the pastor of Newspring, Perry Noble, share about his own bouts with depression, anxiety, and desires to end his ministry and even his life. Pastor Perry set up the conference and brought the man he credited God with to save his ministry to speak to pastors. It was at this conference that I was introduced to Dr. John Walker, who leads the ministry of the Blessing Ranch in Livermore, Colorado. It was at the Blessing Ranch that Pastor Perry and hundreds, even thousands of other pastors found freedom from their own identity crises that led them into all types of dark struggles. I am eternally grateful for their ministry. I am also grateful that while I didn't have the ability to cry out for help, my wife and assistant took the lead in getting me to Dr. John and the Blessing Ranch.

To show you where I was at the time of my visit to the Blessing Ranch in April of 2013, I have included an entry from my journal. At the top of the paper, I simply wrote, "How I Got Here." The following is what was contained in that journal entry.

How I Got Here

I was very strong in faith when we moved into full-time ministry. We saw God do amazing things that got us there, like our business selling in a month. The stresses of ministry were definitely felt then but my faith was strong and I really trusted in God's promises.

I think the first time I really questioned anything was when we left my position as a youth pastor at one church, and moved to another as the Associate Pastor. I was confident because I was so sure I "heard God" tell us to go. When it went south so quickly and there was so much hurt I began to wonder if I had made a mistake. Did I miss God's leading? I began to seriously doubt myself.

It seemed that everything I was confident in was disintegrating. On my 33rd birthday, I found myself in a cabin, miles from nowhere, with a wife and 2 kids, no job, and a "pastor" with no ministry. It was during that time at the cabin that I began to feel great confirmation of my calling as a pastor, and where I felt God gave me a vision for Connection Church. I felt very sure about my calling but was very unsettled about the church. On one hand I felt that the Lord was leading us, but in the back of my mind was the question, "Are you messing up again?"

(With no clear indication I had "messed up" before.) Even after God began to do amazing things, I still worried that I had done the wrong thing. Even a very bad thing (by starting the church). I took a lot of criticism from people in town and at our old church. It hurt deeply and reinforced that what I had done was wrong and I was wrong.

We kept pushing through it all but it took a very heavy toll. I was wiped out before we started and the physical, emotional, and spiritual stress of starting a church, working a full-time job, and finishing my masters didn't refuel my tank and only made things worse.

After a couple of years, I came under a new type of criticism. It was criticism from within the church not from the outside. I was accused of begin a heretic. I was told I preached works based salvation. I was given a book called the Gospel because, "I didn't preach the real Gospel." And I was told I preached a "man-centered gospel" and not a "God-centered gospel." I think, as I reflect on it, that was the beginning of my crisis of faith because everything I believed had been challenged. I had attended churches that had some theological errors (but what church or denomination doesn't). I began to struggle with whether or not I was in error and whether or not I was wrong again and even worse leading people astray.

Another barrage of attacks came about 1-1½ years later that has continued almost consistently ever since. The attackers said that I am very shallow and only preach "the Gospel." So now I have gone from not even knowing the Gospel to only preaching the Gospel that I didn't know. (While we were there, in Colorado, I was asked to think about all the faces of those saved and baptized through the ministry of the church ... I could only see the faces of the critics.) These things coupled with dozens of other criticisms and complaints have made me question everything--even the Truth of Jesus that changed my life and saved my soul.

I now conclude that self-condemnation does not just want to hinder you; it wants to completely destroy you. Its desire is to destroy everything that is good in you and around you. My greatest desire is to trust again. I want to live more in the Truth than I ever have and to be rid of this trap of self-condemnation. Jesus, will you show yourself real in my life again? Will you remove doubt and replace it with trust?

I've had so many people tell me who Jesus is that I don't know anymore. With my default, being that something is wrong with me, I have been convinced by someone that everything I've believed is wrong and therefore nothing can be right.

I just want to know you, Jesus!

But where do I fall between Brennan Manning and David Platt? Matt Chandler and Perry Noble? Mark Driscoll and Steven Furtick?

It's freaking confusing and I just want to know Jesus!

I honestly believe the issue is not a faith crisis as much as an identity crisis. The identity of Jesus and the Father and the Holy Spirit have been so confused by doctrine that I struggle to know what is True. I know the basics of the Gospel. Maybe that's why I never stray from them. But even in regards to how God feels about me I don't have clarity. I think the criticism played right into the hands of my critical, self-condemning nature and said, "See, I told you. You're not good enough, don't measure up, and don't have what it takes for God either."

It's been a long time since I thought of God as smiling and truly taking delight in me. I don't know when the last time was that I read the scripture and saw God's love for me. For so long, I have only seen the work of Jesus on the cross as something God did for himself with me as an afterthought, as though I were a pawn in His cosmic game to gain glory.

It is as if I felt guilty and wrong for delighting in the delight God has for me. Yet it is in my delight of God and His love for me that my heart is transformed and His glory is most clearly seen.

I see how my self-condemnation eroded my confidence in myself, which eroded my confidence in who God is. Because of this, I have not walked in love, lived in love, or lived in God in a long time.

I realize that in all of the work of God that has happened in the church I never once felt like God smiled. I never felt like He delighted in me and took delight in what we were, or are, doing. I think that

is why I've never really stopped to celebrate it. It was
simply, "What do I need to do next, Lord?"

I told my wife three or four times on the Tuesday that these words
were penned that "We should just go home. I cannot change! I have
been this way for thirty-seven years and will be this way when I die.
It's just who I am."

Before you read any further, I want you to stop and think about
how you got to where you are. Identifying with my story is great,
but we need to dig into your own life. What are the them and its of
your life? Who or what has shaped you to be who you are? Take the
time to write your own "How I Got Here" story. For some, it may
go all the way back to childhood, while for others, it may go back
to a significant event in your life. Either way, it is very important
that you do this. Remember, you aren't reading this book to check
it off your list. You are reading this book to discover a better story
for your life. Writing your "How I Got Here" is part of your journey
to a better story.

The Sunday after we got back from Colorado, I watched thirty-five
people celebrate going from death to life in Jesus through baptism in
the parking lot of Statesboro High School, where we were meeting at
the time. We were a church that had grown from seven to over eight
hundred in four and one-half years. We had witnessed hundreds
of salvations and baptisms. We were seeing Jesus put lives back
together. Yet, it was at these baptisms that I, for the first time in all
those years, felt God was smiling, saying, "Well done. You are my
son with whom I am well pleased!"

There is hope!

I am freer than I have ever been. I am enjoying ministry more than
I ever have. I did not say I no longer have battles. I do. God did not

change my circumstances; God changed me. I still have battles. The difference is I have learned how to win the battles that I fight.

I don't know the outcome of my life and how God will use me. But I know He has a plan, and I am securely in the hands of a loving Father in whom I take great delight and who takes great delight in me! How have I been able to find a new freedom that is removed from years of identity crisis, self-condemnation, and performance-based living? I became convinced that God had a better story.

I hope my story will in some way encourage you. Understand that I am not a special case, and God is not just writing a better story for my life. He desires to write a better story for all who will allow Him to take over the pen. He has written this promise with the blood of His Son, and the fulfillment of His promise of a better story is surer than the sun coming up tomorrow.

Now, let's look at the life of someone else who gives us hope that even amid difficult and painful circumstances, God still has a better story for our lives.

CHAPTER 3

❖

A BETTER STORY?

Have you ever been amazed at the way someone's value seems to increase once he or she dies? Admittedly, that's probably the worst intro to a chapter in the history of books. But even at funerals, we hear people memorialized as amazing even when they were jerks their entire lives. The way we cut out parts of their lives and just jump to the good parts reminds me of the power of editing videos. We use videos a lot in our church, and I have been amazed at how well our video guys are able to take what seemed to be horrible footage and turn it into gold.

I vividly remember the first time we did a video shoot for our church. We wanted to do a five-week introduction to our Connect Groups, which is what we call our small groups. You have to understand, when your name is Connection Church, everything you do has to have "connect" in it somewhere. Shooting these videos was one of the most awkward moments of my life. I think I would have rather had a tooth filled than do those videos. The first video we shot was at a friend's house. He has three children and also has to be at work around 6 a.m. That dynamic is what caused the experience to be such a pressure cooker! We had to shoot the video after his children went to bed, so we wouldn't be a distraction to their regular routine.

That was the rock. I also knew my buddy had to be up at 5 a.m. for work, and we couldn't keep him up all night. That was the hard place.

Somewhere between the rock and the hard place was my dreadful ability to speak on camera. It took what seemed to be forever to get the footage for a four-minute video. I could sense the aggravation I felt with myself was only the tip of the iceberg in comparison to the aggravation the others involved felt.

I don't believe I'll be getting a call to co-star alongside Johnny Depp anytime soon, but to my surprise, the video turned out pretty well in comparison to what I gave them to work with.

In the same way, we often want to tell a better story about people than what they actually lived by editing out the things that aren't appealing about them. This tendency is also true when it comes to how we view our Bible heroes. We sometimes forget that David was an adulterer, Moses was a murderer (as was Paul), Abraham allowed other men to pay him in exchange for sex with his wife more than once, and Peter refused to eat with people because of their race. Those stories will make you feel a little better about yourself! Another biblical hero whose successes are often exalted without fully recognizing his failures is Joseph.

I'm sure many of you grew up talking about Joseph's "coat of many colors," his dreams of grandeur and purpose, and how he rescued his family from the grips of famine. What we often leave out are the struggles he went through. They include living with ten brothers who hated his guts to the point of wanting to kill him and being at the brink of death after being thrown into an empty cistern by those same brothers. Joseph was also sold into slavery and taken to a foreign country. Once he was in the foreign land (Egypt), Joseph was purchased by a man named Potiphar.

Potiphar, a well-to-do Egyptian official, brought Joseph into his home as a slave. As Potiphar observed Joseph, he realized the hand of God was upon his life. Because everything Joseph did prospered, Potiphar put him in charge of his whole household. Joseph excelled. In Joseph's mind, he had to think, *I have finally gotten my feet under me. God is finally going to fulfill the dreams he gave me.*

Those thoughts were short-lived as Potiphar's wife attempted to seduce Joseph. He rejected her, so she framed him as having tried to seduce her. Even though Joseph resisted temptation and sought to honor God and Potiphar, he still ended up in prison.

While in prison, Joseph interpreted the dreams of the pharaoh's cupbearer and baker. Both of these men were locked up for undisclosed events that caused Pharaoh's wrath to burn against them. The cupbearer went on to be restored to his position, while the baker was hanged. Even though Joseph had asked the cupbearer to remember him as he went before Pharaoh, Joseph was forgotten. This was just another opportunity for Joseph to sink into despair and doubt.

Joseph's life seemed to be a rerun. It was a continuous bad dream that just wouldn't stop. For him, *they* were his brothers. Or *they* could have been something as simple as seeing a father and son walking the streets of Egypt. Seeing them was a reminder that he could no longer see his own father. *It* was possibly the smell of death in the prison cell, reminding him that his old life in Canaan was dead, and literal death could come for him at any time.

The cupbearer finally remembered Joseph when Pharaoh was dreadfully troubled by dreams that no one else could interpret. Joseph was eventually called before Pharaoh, and upon interpreting his dreams, he was appointed to the highest position in the kingdom, second only to Pharaoh himself.

It's easy to imagine how, even after gaining his freedom from jail, Joseph would have been taken back to his emotional imprisonment in a moment. It is as if the physical prison in Egypt was a metaphor for Joseph's life. Even after rising to power as Pharaoh's right-hand man, how could he not live his life on pins and needles, just waiting for the next collapse? Was Joseph a biblical hero? Absolutely! Was his life void of pain, distress, and trouble? Absolutely not!

When we look at the end of Joseph's life in Genesis 50:15–26, we see a man who was able to offer forgiveness, had no regrets, and was still clinging to and proclaiming the promises of God. I think you will find these verses to be remarkable if you reflect on all Joseph went through as you read them.

> When Joseph's brothers saw that their father was dead, they said, "What if Joseph holds a grudge against us and pays us back for all the wrongs we did to him?" So they sent word to Joseph, saying, "Your father left these instructions before he died: 'This is what you are to say to Joseph: I ask you to forgive your brothers the sins and the wrongs they committed in treating you so badly.' Now please forgive the sins of the servants of the God of your father." When their message came to him, Joseph wept.
>
> His brothers then came and threw themselves down before him. "We are your slaves," they said.
>
> But Joseph said to them "Don't be afraid. Am I in the place of God? You intended to harm me, but God intended it for good to accomplish what is now being done, the saving of many lives. So then, don't

be afraid. I will provide for you and your children."
And he reassured them and spoke kindly to them.

Joseph stayed in Egypt, along with all his father's
family. He lived a hundred and ten years and saw
the third generation of Ephraim's children. Also the
children of Makir son of Manasseh were placed at
birth on Joseph's knees.

Then Joseph said to his brothers, "I am about to die.
But God will surely come to your aid and take you
up out of this land to the land he promised on oath
to Abraham, Isaac and Jacob." And Joseph made
the Israelites swear an oath and said, "God will
surely come to your aid, and then you must carry
my bones up from this place."

So Joseph died at the age of a hundred and ten.
And after they embalmed him, he was placed in a
coffin in Egypt.

How did he make it? Through all of the prisons and pain, how did
he finish with a great story? How did he forgive those who hurt him
so much? After so much disappointment, how did he still trust so
heavily in the promises of God?

I believe it was because Joseph never lost sight of who he was. Joseph
had the great privilege of knowing the love of his earthly father. He
was shaped by the fact that his dad loved him, believed in him, and
even while he may have outwardly rebuked him for his God-given
dream, inwardly he recognized something special about Joseph. The
love of his earthly father shaped his identity by giving him a sense
of value and worth.

Joseph also knew the love of his heavenly Father. He had been given dreams early in life that he was able to recognize as coming from God. They were not the outflow of drinking too much Mountain Dew, or watching a horror film and going to bed to dream some crazy dream. They were of divine origin and a word straight from the Lord that would serve as a life preserver when storms raged on the sea of life. Joseph was armed with an identity that came from his earthly father and his heavenly Father. It was an identity that was good and true, and it kept him from drowning in a sea of despair.

Before we go any further, I want to acknowledge that many, if not most, of us are lacking at least one of these influences in our lives. We either didn't have the assurance of value and worth that came from a parent or caregiver, or we have never really felt loved by our heavenly Father. For some of us, the lack of the first has prevented the presence of the second. Don't worry! We will address all of this. Right now, I just want you to see that an accurate, true, God-given identity has the power to lift us from the prison to the palace, which is where we, the children of the King, should live.

Back to Joseph. How did he do it? How did he forgive such great offense? How did he get to the end of his life and speak the words we find in Genesis 50:19–21 and 24–25? How did the apostle Paul pen the liberated words of Romans 8 when he had lived in the cycle of sin and condemnation he writes about in the previous chapter (Romans 7:14–25)?

They all became convinced that God had a better story! Neither Joseph nor Paul knew all the details nor how the story would ultimately be written. But they knew God had a story to write and that it was good.

The story God was and is writing through each of our lives is the gospel story. The gospel does not begin in Bethlehem in a manger, and it does not end on a cross outside of Jerusalem or even with an empty tomb. The gospel is as eternal as God. It is without beginning and without end.

When we surrender our lives to God, we are giving Him the pen, relinquishing our wills to His as He writes a better story—His story—through us. It is a story of anguish and delight, sorrow and joy, failure and triumph. Yet within the boundaries of His story, we discover who we are, and most importantly, we discover whose we are.

Joseph, through all of the prisons and all of the pain, got to the end of his life with no regrets. He got to the end of his life so sure of the faithfulness of God that he was able to say, "I have one request. Don't leave my bones in this pagan nation! When God gives you the land He has promised, and He will, bury me there!"

In his prisons, Joseph knew the story wasn't finished. He knew there was more to be written. God had not put down the pen. He has not put down the pen with your life, either. There is a better story for you, and it is submerged in God's story ... the gospel!

Your first step in this process is simply to believe. Believe a better story is possible. Rebuke the mindset that says you cannot change. That is a lie. It is not grounded in the truth!

At the end of my experience at the Blessing Ranch, Dr. Walker asked me how I was feeling about our progress and returning home. I replied, "Cautiously optimistic." Wow! "Cautiously optimistic?" That's all I had. My desire was to want to climb on the roof and shout, "I am free!" But that wasn't what I felt. I was more like a skittish dog that had been kicked too many times by an abusive owner. Even after it has been placed in a new home, it takes days, weeks, or months before the dog can really begin to trust its new owners. Condemnation had been the abusive owner of my heart and emotions, and it would take a season of days and weeks before I could fully trust that I was free. Cycles of struggle followed by slight improvement and thoughts of, *Now I've really got it figured out,* had dumped me in a pit of despair so many times that I didn't know if I had really changed. Or, more accurately, if God's Word truly had the power to change me.

It took me four days to get to cautiously optimistic. I am asking you to do it in three short chapters! I am depending greatly on the power of God's Spirit to convince you this is possible. I am asking you to trust me when I tell you that it is possible. Yes, even possible for you!

This is what I know; if you grab hold of the principles given to us through scripture and put into practice the things you will read in the next few chapters, you will experience the truth of Jesus's words in John 8:31–32.

> To the Jews who had believed him, Jesus said, "If you hold to my teaching, you are really my disciples. Then you will know the truth, and the *truth will set you free.* (emphasis mine)

If you are willing to simply say, "I am cautiously optimistic," you have all the faith you need at this point to move to chapter 4. In fact, whether you realize it or not, you have enough faith to begin moving the mountain of condemnation and pulling up the roots of your false identity.

> I tell you the truth, if you have *faith as small as a mustard seed,* you can say to this *mountain,* "Move from here to there" and it will move. *Nothing* will be impossible for you. (Matthew 17:20b; emphasis mine)

The apostles said to the Lord, "Increase our faith!"

He replied, "If you have *faith as small as a mustard seed*, you can say to this mulberry tree, 'Be *uprooted* and planted in the sea,' and it will obey you." (Luke 17:5–6; emphasis mine)

CHAPTER 4

◆

STUCK

I felt terrible for the little guy. He seemed to be abandoned and was obviously lost. I'm not sure how he got there. I'm not 100 percent sure he knew how he got there. I'm not sure he knew how much trouble he was in.

It was easy to see he was in an almost helpless and hopeless situation. No matter which direction he turned, it most likely wasn't going to end well for him. He had no options. To put it plainly, he was stuck! I couldn't be of much help. The flow of traffic was moving way too fast for me to stop. To do that would have put others in danger. Helplessly, I had to keep moving, leaving him to a fate that I would never know.

This story took place one day as I was headed to Savannah, Georgia, from my home in Statesboro. Not long into my journey along the interstate, I looked over into the median and saw a black dog. He was walking with his head down, seemingly distracted, but there had to be some recognition of the seriousness of his situation. There were cars zooming by on each side, at eighty miles per hour. In order to reach safety, he had to cross two lanes of traffic. There really wasn't much I could do but hope that he would somehow make it across.

I wonder how many of us feel like that dog. Stuck. Lost. Abandoned. Even helpless and hopeless. We're not sure how we got to where we are, but we're absolutely sure the place where we are is not where we need to be. Sometimes we're also good at putting our head down, looking busy, and acting distracted, while the whole time we feel stuck. In our minds, probably lurking in the depths of the subconscious, we wonder, *How did I get here?* Have you ever stopped acting like everything is okay long enough to truly ask and answer that question?

Truthfully, how did you get to where you are? How did condemnation take such a hold on your life? Why did you begin to take such an unpopular view of yourself? Why did you begin to doubt you could make a difference? When did a false identity begin to take over your heart? At what point did you quit believing God has a better story for you?

You must understand that before you can overcome a false identity, you must recognize where it came from. I will go ahead and lay my cards on the table and tell you that if the information shaping how you see yourself does not line up with the truth of what God says about you, it's a lie, no matter the source of the information.

Sources of influence that surround us constantly input data and information into our minds and hearts. We have to realize that while there are influences that *cause* us to be the way we are, those influences are not *excuses* for why we are the way we are. The old adage, "This is just the way I am," is an excuse for us to remain in darkness, but it cannot stand in the light of God's truth.

What seems to be reality because of the incoming data creates perceptions of who we are in our minds and hearts. From these perceptions we draw conclusions about ourselves, others, and God.

Inaccurate conclusions affect every area of our lives. We are impacted relationally, emotionally, spiritually, and physically.

A large sore spot developed in my life during a two-month stint of ministry as an associate pastor. I alluded to it briefly in my "How Did I Get Here" journal entry. (I'm trusting you did yours like you were instructed.) It still amazes me how much this short two-month season of ministry affected my life. It began when I left a solid youth ministry position to go help a friend of mine who was a senior pastor. The plan was for me to be his associate. I was especially excited about this because not only was he a good friend, he was also my mentor. He called himself my "spiritual father," and we spent much time working out and eating lunches while talking about ministry. There were signs from the beginning that some things weren't exactly right. Even though not everything added up, and there seemed to be some character issues, I overlooked them because of his charisma and ministry gifting.

The character questions I had swept under the rug for so long became impossible to ignore once I was fully engrained in the fabric of "his" church. One of my jobs was paying the bills, and I quickly saw abuses with the money. It was apparent that I was there to write the checks, make the deposits, and not ask questions. However, my conscience was killing me. There were also promises that I saw him make to the congregation and others that would never even be attempted to be fulfilled. As more and more things began to come into the light, I began to realize I had stepped into a bad situation.

The first thought that began to plague me and create the sore spot was questioning myself about how I missed God's leading. Hindsight is 20/20, and looking back, I realize I was exactly where I was supposed to be. However, in that moment, I felt like a fool for dragging my wife and children away from a great ministry position only to land in the middle of what seemed to be hell. This question haunted me even as we started Connection because the thought in my mind was always, *Am I really following God, or am I making a mistake?* This haunted me for years even when we saw God do miracle after miracle through the ministry at Connection Church.

The second irritant that quickly worked its way into a sore spot was when he began to question my integrity and motives. A couple of weeks after I got to his church the pastor came in and told me, in tears, that God had spoken to him, and I was supposed to take his place as the senior pastor. It was a shock to me, but I knew I was there to help him in whatever he needed me to do. His plan was to step back and oversee this church and three others. I simply reassured him I was there to do whatever he needed me to do.

Over the next couple of weeks, I didn't hear a lot about the plan to transition the leadership of the church to other people. When I asked about it, I was told that, "This is my church, and I'm not just going to hand it over to someone." Wow! Can you see how things quickly got confusing? It was shortly after that conversation that I was accused of trying to take over the church. It was so disheartening because, to be honest, I had no desire to be in that particular town. I was only there because I felt God wanted me to help him. The accusations continued. Every time I asked questions, they were turned back around in a way that made it look like I was the bad guy with a bad heart. I was even told that I, "acted like a fatherless son"; this is a cleaned-up version of what he really said. I spent hours talking to two of my best friends, trying to figure out what I was doing wrong. What I now realize is that narcissistic people never accept that they are wrong and are the best at turning their mistakes into your mistakes. This pastor was the best I've ever seen at doing this.

The third contributor to this sore spot came in the degrading of my gifting and the questioning of my calling. I was told, "If you ever hope to pastor a church, you will have to learn to preach better because no one would want to hear you the way you are." Do you think that could cause an issue for someone who has always felt loved and accepted based on how well he or she performed? This caused pain in my life from that day forward—until I got to the Blessing Ranch. I couldn't shake those words from my heart and mind, even when people came back week after week and brought others with them to the services at our church. On top of that, my calling to preach and pastor was questioned through statements like, "Not everyone is called to preach every week. If I could get you to understand that things would be better." There was never one time that I had asked to preach.

There were more encounters like this than I can recount here in this section. I can tell you at this point in my life, everything was so confusing. I was to the point of thinking things would never make sense again. I can remember exactly where I was the day I heard in my mind, *None of the dreams you've ever had will ever come true!* I really thought it was over, not only for me as a pastor, but in all of life.

The pain I experienced through this short season of ministry impacted every area of my life. I removed myself from relationships. I was physically present but mentally and emotionally absent. I went into a depression that is still being resolved to this day. I questioned everything spiritually because I wondered if anything I learned from this person was true. I literally had to spend months ciphering through "truths" I had learned in order to find solid footing in the truth of the Bible. Physically, I had migraines and even had to sleep with a plastic mouthpiece so that I would not grind my teeth. My jaws were so exhausted from the tension that I couldn't even chew gum. I had a long way to go if I was going to escape the false identity that had been established through all of my experiences.

To explore this further, let's go back and take another look at the life of Joseph, this time from a little different angle. After I gave a message on the first two chapters of this book at our church, a good friend asked me, "What if you are like the brothers?" His question was followed with the statement, "That's how I felt during the message." He is a great friend, but sometimes he likes to deflect the love of God by finding ways the messages don't apply to him.

My response was, "You are absolutely like the brothers. You never felt loved or affirmed by your father, and because of that, you couldn't receive the love of your heavenly Father or anyone else." For once, he really didn't have a comeback.

We saw in the previous chapters some influences that helped shape a healthy identity within Joseph. The influence of his father's love, as well as that of his heavenly Father, provided proof of his value and worth and gave him a sense of purpose that was greater than himself. It's great that Joseph had all of that, but what about those who never had a father to affirm their worth? What about those of us who never had a dream in which God told us we had a purpose and confirmed the value He saw in us?

I believe more of us find ourselves in the place of the brothers than in the place of Joseph. Joseph and Benjamin were born to Jacob through Rachel, the love of his life (Genesis 29). The others were born to him through Leah, whom Jacob was tricked into marrying through a bait and switch by her father and two servants, Zilpah and Bilhah. I know it sounds like good material for a new reality show, but this was the experience of the brothers and a powerful force in shaping their identities.

Think about it. The source of the brothers' identities was that they were sons of women their father never really loved. They were loved less than Joseph and Benjamin, the youngest of the brothers. There was no elaborate coat. There were no dreams. There was nothing to indicate they had value, worth, or purpose. What a drastic contrast to the life of Joseph!

What about you? Even if it was not the absence of a loving father, there have been other influences that have shaped the way we see ourselves. The scenarios we talked about in chapter 1 may be the sore spot that causes us to fold like a wilted flower every time it gets pushed. But influences have infiltrated our experiences that cause us to develop that sore spot. Through the incoming data of our experiences, we begin to believe things about ourselves that may or may not be true according to the greatest truth, God's Word. If we can identify those sources, and identify the lies we have believed, we can refute them with God's truth and establish an accurate identity for ourselves. Let's take a look at some of those influences or sources of input data.

Major Events

Eleven years ago, my dad was in a terrible motorcycle wreck that changed his life and my family's lives forever. Since that time, he has battled to regain the same quality of life that he had before the wreck. It seems that every time he starts to get better, something else happens. He has had over fifteen surgeries on his left leg alone and finally had it amputated in August of 2011. He recently had a brain hemorrhage that nearly took his life. I have watched him live in pain for the last eleven years, many days not being able to get out of bed. Dad's struggle is an experience that has greatly influenced our lives. Many people would call it a defining moment.

We experience thousands of things each day. Yet there are those major events in our lives that have the potential to define us. Some of these are very painful and leave us with wounds that speak lies from the deepest part of who we are.

How about you? Has an event in your life been a defining moment for you? Something that happened that has left you wondering and questioning ever since, even doubting yourself and your value and worth?

You may read about my dad's story and think, *At least you still have your dad. All I got was a phone call that he was gone.* Maybe you have experienced the great pain of an unexpected loss of a wife, husband, son, daughter, mother, or father. Would you say that the moment of the call or visit was a defining moment and shaping influence for you? I bet in some way it changed the way you viewed yourself or the way you viewed God.

Amid the grief we wonder if God really loves us. There is a condemnation that develops within our hearts as we ponder that question. We struggle with authentic joy and happiness because we feel guilt for having it. It is as if experiencing joy and no longer being defined by the tragedy invalidates the pain of our loved ones, or somehow the memory will be lost. It won't! That is a lie.

We often take the tragedies of our lives and transpose them to God, allowing them to shape and distort His identity. Since God is the image bearer from whom we get our own identity, once the identity of God has been distorted, we are no longer able to find a clear identity for ourselves. The false identities we develop from an inaccurate identity of God begin to lie to us and tell us we are defined by the tragedy. The tragedy becomes our identity.

Maybe it wasn't *someone* who was robbed from you, but it was *something*. Your identity began to change because your dignity, purity, innocence, or all three were taken from you. Maybe the event was rape or physical abuse. Maybe you went through the horror of molestation. Perhaps it was someone you trusted deeply who hurt you the most. It's the people that we let deepest into our hearts that have the potential to cause us the greatest pain.

You've blocked everyone out because your experience has taught you that true, unconditional love doesn't really exist. Your mind and heart seem to resonate that somehow you aren't clean. Your soul is stained, and it can't be made whole again. If you were to be honest, you would define yourself as damaged goods. That too is a lie! A lie you've been taught by your experience, not by God.

Maybe it was a loss of employment or a failure in some venture. When your job disappeared or the venture died, so did a part of you. Now you struggle. All you see yourself as is a failure because your experience seems to be clear that you are. Whatever the event may have been, it has shaped your life and your identity by giving you a lens of experience through which you view yourself.

Through all that went on with my dad, I have had some serious conversations with God, trying to figure out why. I still don't have an answer. I have become more and more comfortable answering "God questions" with, "I don't know." His ways and thoughts are higher than ours. How can I fathom what is in the mind and plans of God? When I don't know the answer, I always go back to what I do know, and what I do know gives me strength and faith to take my next step.

This is what I know: God is good. God is sovereign. God is faithful. I can trust Him. I cannot look at the cross without seeing His goodness. The cross is the pinnacle of God's goodness that rises higher than humanity's entire calamity. I cannot look at creation without seeing that He is sovereignly in control. I cannot look at all the fulfillment of His promises without seeing that He is faithful. When I realize all of them are true, I am left with only one conclusion. I can trust Him. So can you! You don't need enough trust to take ten steps. You only need enough trust to take your next step.

Culture

We are constantly bombarded with commercials, sitcoms, reality shows, movies, billboards, tweets, blogs, and Facebook messages that tell us who we're supposed to be. So many have bought into the lie that the size of your breasts or waistline determines your value or worth. For some, it's led to anorexia, bulimia, or some other eating disorder. Now you deal not only with condemnation of "not looking good enough" but also with the guilt of struggling with an eating disorder. The lie you believe is that you have to do this to be loved. I tell you that you were loved before you breathed your first breath! Jesus does not love you based on the size of your dress or your chest. He loves you because He loves you! That says so much and yet leaves so much unexplained. Even though it is incomprehensible, God loves us just because He loves us!

Culture told some of you, "If you don't have sex before marriage, you don't fit in. You're going to be the forty-year-old virgin. Something's wrong with you." So you decided to give your purity away. Then the culture that promised acceptance if you started having sex turned on you and began to make you feel cheap because you did have sex. Now, since you've cheapened yourself, why not just have sex with whoever, whenever. Even though you may laugh it off or hide it somewhere inside, you feel like damaged goods. You feel irreparable and broken. That, too, is a lie, but the sore spot kicks in anytime you're reminded of what you've done and those you've done it with.

Culture tells the guys that if they aren't having sex with as many girls as they can, they aren't men. It tells you that if you don't objectify women and view them as a KFC bucket—only as breasts, thighs, and legs—something's wrong with you. You pursue sex because of your own identity crisis and, in the meantime, contribute to theirs. The lie you believe is that this is the way it's supposed to be, and it's just who you are.

For others, culture told you to be loved and accepted you had to use and abuse drugs and alcohol. Or you believed the lie that the only way to escape the pain of an event or experience was to numb the pain. Once the pills or bottle sunk its claws into you, it tore you apart rather than build you up. Now your identity is first and foremost addict or drunk. That is a lie if you are in Christ. God says you are a new creation, a saint in Christ, who still struggles with alcohol or drugs. If you are in Christ, neither alcohol or drugs has the power to define you.

You'll never find out who you truly are from someone who wants something from you. You will only find out who he or she needs you to be. Our modern culture is trying to brand you with its identity so that it may prosper at your expense. The amazing thing about God is that He needs nothing you have, so we know that His motives aren't tainted. He simply loves you.

Primary Influencers

If you are a perfect parent, you need to skip the story I'm about to tell you so that you won't think I'm a complete loser. If you are like me and try really hard to be a godly parent but muddle it up sometimes, you'll be able to relate to what I'm about to tell you. If you don't have kids, this will be a lesson in what not to do just in case you one day decide to enter into the most amazingly frustrating, unbelievable blessing known as parenting.

For us, mornings during the school year can get really hectic. One Friday morning, this was especially the case. I was in a hurry to get out the door, get all three kids in my truck, and get them all to school on time. Once we piled into the vehicle, I hurriedly began to back out of the driveway. The only problem was the back door wasn't closed. On the side of our driveway sat a basketball goal, which thankfully was on a portable base, not the permanent kind that is cemented into the ground. As I sped backward, the door caught the basketball goal and knocked it onto the side of the truck. As it slid down the bed of the truck, I think my blood pressure went to 340/250. All I can say is I lost it! I lit into my children for not closing the door. I think I even threatened to throw the basketball goal away. (As if it were the basketball goal's fault!) My temper ran hot, and I didn't hide it in any way.

I really blew up that whole experience as a dad, and unfortunately, there are countless other stories I could tell. My thoughts kept going back to what my children would tell their therapists one day! Later that day, I put my arm around my oldest son and told him, "Hey, buddy, I'm sorry we had a bad morning."

He replied, "It's okay."

I told him, "I try really hard to be a good dad. I just mess it up a lot."

To which he only smiled as if to say, "I know." I'm still not sure if his smile was to say, "I know you try really hard to be a good dad, and I'm grateful," or, "I know you mess it up a lot." Most likely it was both!

The last area of influence and experience we will look at is our parents and those who were a consistent, shaping presence in our life. These are the people who primarily shaped our view of life and our view of us. How these people related to us, talked to us, and viewed us became a large part of how we view ourselves. The character and attributes of these people are typically transposed onto God so that we view God, to some degree, as having the same character and attributes as they do.

For example, if you had a father who had a "drill sergeant" mentality and constantly critiqued your every move, finding plenty of things to criticize and little to affirm, your view of God probably leans heavily toward Him as critical and judgmental, not loving and compassionate. You would see performance and "being good enough" as the way to gain God's love. When your performance fails, you feel His love has left you.

The experience I shared earlier about a previous church I was at and the hurt I experienced is just one example of many that I recognize shaped my life and created a sore spot in my heart. As crazy as it sounds, I realize now that I transposed how that pastor described me onto God and even began to feel like that was how God saw me. The old saying, "Sticks and stones may break my bones, but words will never hurt me," is simply not true! Words are powerful, and they are able to shape our perceived identities and, ultimately, the way we live out of that identity.

My bad church experience (Don't we all have one?) was a huge obstacle for me to overcome in order to see who I am in Christ and to fulfill the purposes God has given me. This experience left a "them" and an "it" in my life. I honestly didn't know if I would ever overcome it. I was afraid my deceitfully wicked heart was lying to me when I checked it for where I was wrong in the relationship. Every issue was my fault, and even when I thought I saw solid ground to stand on and plead my case, it quickly eroded under my feet.

The list of influences that have shaped us could go on and on because no one is perfect, and we live in a world that constantly reminds us of our imperfections. In regards to my role as a father, I'm not perfect. I cannot perfectly reflect the love of God to my children, so I consistently point them to Him and try to get them to see who they are in Him. Knowing who we are in Him is the only way we will ever consistently overcome who the world tells us we are and should be.

We are surrounded by imperfect influences that, to some degree, give us all a false identity. So what should we do? Run and hide? Live alone on a mountain? Lock ourselves in a closet? No! We are not called to run from the world but to go into the world and change it.

As I mentioned earlier, most of us find ourselves in the place of Joseph's brothers. We have developed false identities because of imperfect, or bad, influences. And many of us have never been sure that God really loves us and has a plan for our lives.

Again, we cannot completely shield ourselves from all influences of the culture around us. Culture tells us so many lies, and we can't protect ourselves from the world that is pushing its identity on us. But we can establish an identity that is greater than the one the world tries to give us! What we must do is establish an identity that trumps the one the world pushes on us.

We must consider the major experiences of our lives as we begin to identify the false identity that we've accepted. We must investigate our experiences in order to understand why we are the way we are. What has shaped our views of God and ourselves? What have I believed about myself and others that is simply not true? Then I must bring it into the light of God's truth, exposing it once and for all, rendering it powerless to hold me captive to a false identity any longer.

So what is the identity of those of us who identify with Joseph's brothers more than with Joseph himself? We must understand that the entire Bible points us to Jesus. The account of Joseph's life shows us a shadow of the redeemer that God planned to send in order to, once and for all, save His people. Look at the great forgiveness Joseph extends to his brothers as they stand before him, vulnerable and naked, deserving judgment.

We must see that God had grace, forgiveness, and purpose for the brothers as well as for Joseph. He made them into a great nation. They were His people. They were the people who would pave the way for the Messiah. He had *a better story* for the brothers as well. God has a better story for you.

CHAPTER 5

FOUR TRUTHS FROM THE BOAT

Regardless of what experience has taught you or how unmovable your mountain may seem, we should not lose hope. Our God is bigger than the mountains we face. Many times, if we are observant, we are able to learn things from the experiences of others.

The best sources from which we are able to learn from the life experiences of others is the Bible. Hebrews 12:1 tells us,

> Therefore, since we are surrounded by such a great cloud of witnesses, let us throw off everything that hinders and the sin that so easily entangles, and let us run with perseverance the race marked out for us.

The "cloud of witnesses" is the great men and women of God mentioned in what is often called "the Hall of Faith" (Hebrews 11). This text is often interpreted to mean that Abraham, Moses, David, and the like are somewhere, watching the things we are doing. What the writer of Hebrews is actually saying is that the lives of these saints are testimonies to us of the power of God and how we should respond in trust and obedience to Him. Their stories are testimonies to the fact that, even in the worst of circumstances, we can trust God and continue moving forward because He has a better story for our lives.

There may not be a better Bible hero to learn from than the apostle Peter. His story is one of boneheaded mistakes. It is a story of the power of God to overcome those mistakes and use the least likely of us. There is no greater example of this than the account we find in Matthew 14:22–36.

> Immediately he made the disciples get into the boat and go before him to the other side, while he dismissed the crowds. And after he had dismissed the crowds, he went up on the mountain by himself to pray. When evening came, he was there alone, but the boat by this time was a long way from the land, beaten by the waves, for the wind was against them. And in the fourth watch of the night he came to them, walking on the sea. But when the disciples saw him walking on the sea, they were terrified, and said, "It is a ghost!" and they cried out in fear. But immediately Jesus spoke to them, saying, "Take heart; it is I. Do not be afraid."
>
> And Peter answered him, "Lord, if it is you, command me to come to you on the water." He said, "Come." So Peter got out of the boat and walked on the water and came to Jesus. But when he saw the wind, he was afraid, and beginning to sink he cried out, "Lord, save me." Jesus immediately reached out his hand and took hold of him, saying to him, "O you of little faith, why did you doubt?" And when they got into the boat, the wind ceased. And those

in the boat worshiped him, saying, "Truly you are the Son of God."

And when they had crossed over, they came to land at Gennesaret. And when the men of that place recognized him, they sent around to that entire region and brought to him all who were sick and implored him that they might only touch the fringe of his garment. And as many as touched it were made well.

This had to be one of Peter's "How did I get here?" moments. That thought had to cross his mind when he felt himself sinking into the raging sea. "I've done it again," had to be running laps through his head in that moment. This was just one in a long list of difficult lessons Peter had to learn.

Dr. John Walker, out at the Blessing Ranch, phrased it this way: "Your 'stuff' doesn't disqualify you. It only shows you where God would like to bring his grace, comfort, and mercy into your life more fully."

It's interesting that Peter cried out to Jesus, "Lord, if it's you, tell me to come to you on the water." Peter seems to be inquiring about the identity of Jesus, but I believe Peter's desire to walk on water had more to do with Peter's identity. To walk upon the water was a sign that Peter was accepted. He was good enough. He was even superior to the other disciples. To sink meant that He was ordinary. Nothing special. Perhaps loved, but not in an extraordinary way. Peter sank. The experience with the waves exposed Peter's weakness but became a testimony to Jesus's strength. Both Jesus and Peter were on top of the water as they went back to the boat. It is in Jesus that we find the power to overcome the storms of life's experience and see clearly who Jesus is and who we are.

Peter had to learn that his identity would only be secure in the power of Christ. It could not and would not be established through Peter's own strength, effort, or ability. This was a hard lesson for Peter to learn and an even harder one for him to accept. But through his experience, we are taught some powerful truths. Truths that can help us rest in God's story for our life and find security in our identities in Christ. We must learn the same lesson as Peter, or we will continue to take the same test over and over again.

It's also interesting that the disciples weren't expecting Jesus to show up. As we look back in hindsight, we have the luxury of knowing from the gospel of Mark, chapter 6, verse 48, that they were never out of the sight of Jesus. But the disciples didn't realize He was even aware of their circumstances. It's easy for us, like the disciples, to feel like God isn't aware of the depth of our despair. We wrestle with the question, "Does God even know what I'm going through?" We sense that Jesus doesn't know, doesn't care, or is unmoved by our plights.

The first truth you have to learn from these scriptures and dozens, even hundreds like them, is that Jesus knows where you are. He's never taken His eyes off you, and He is much more interested in helping you than you are probably willing to accept. You must get this into your heart, so you can believe it with your mind. Jesus knows where you are in life. He knows the pain you feel. He has even experienced it Himself. Hebrews 4:15 tells us,

> For we do not have a high priest [Jesus] who is
> unable to sympathize with our weaknesses, but we
> have one who has been tempted in every way, just
> as we are —yet was without sin.

Jesus not only knows where you are, He understands where you are. In fact, He has been where you are. He knows what it is to suffer great loss. He watched as all who were created through Him plummeted into destruction through the disobedience of His prize creation. He knows what it is to feel physical pain. He felt the pain of nails pierce His hands and feet, and the skin and muscle from His back be torn apart by repeated flogging. He took our sins. He has felt our temptations. He has experienced it all, not just the socially acceptable sins.

He knows how it feels to be betrayed by those you love as He was betrayed by one in His inner circle, Judas. He knows the feelings of anxiety that come with facing the unknown as His sweat literally turned to blood as He prayed, awaiting the arrival of those who would hand Him over to be crucified. He has felt the pain of separation as He was separated from His heavenly Father as God's wrath for our sins was poured out on Him. You can fill in any situation that comes to mind, but the truth remains the same: He knows!

As I read this account in Matthew 14, I don't think the disciples really thought Jesus would or could come to the rescue. It's interesting to note that the disciples didn't even recognize Him. I imagine it was for several reasons. There was probably mist or rain in the air, blurring their vision. The height of the waves probably made His figure go in and out of view. There's no telling how dark it was at night, in a storm, on the sea. I also believe it was hard for them to recognize Him because they didn't expect to see Him.

This is where we often find ourselves. We wonder, *Is God willing to help me?* And then, if we finally convince ourselves that He is willing, we wonder, *Is He even able to help me?* These are some of the questions I was asking in Colorado. If someone had asked me those questions in regards to themselves, I would have affirmed how faithful God is. But for some reason, it is much more difficult for us to believe He is able to help us than it is to believe He can help others. It's easy for us to believe that Jesus is much more involved in the lives of others than He is in our lives.

This is why truth #2 is so important – Jesus is never as far away as you think He is. When they couldn't make it any further, He was there. In my own life, when I finally got to the end of myself, He was waiting with the pen to write a better story. He has a better story waiting for you as well if you are finally ready to let go of the pen, and give Him your life as a blank sheet of paper to write His story for you.

In Matthew 14:34, we are told, "When they had crossed over, they landed at Gennesaret." This is truth #3: Jesus always gets us to the other side.

It's hard to shake ourselves from the demonstrative statement we've either knowingly or unknowingly adopted as our lives' mission statement: "I will never get beyond this!" The truth of God's Word is that He will always get us to the other side of the tempests in our lives if we simply let Him get into the boat. He will write a better story if we simply give Him the pen. This was true for the disciples, and it is true for us as well. None of the experiences we've had, which includes those things we have done as well as those things that have been done to us, is able to speak a final word over us when we are in Christ.

This experience must have brought Peter to a new level of highs and lows. Can you sense the exhilaration that Peter felt when the sea turned solid under his feet? It was that moment of realization that spoke to his heart, "Jesus is who He says He is. I am loved, accepted, and special to Him." Yet we can feel, and unfortunately more easily identify, with what he must have felt as the circumstances that surrounded him seemed to verify what his heart had sensed all of his life: "You're not extraordinary. Love is only skin deep. There really is nothing special about you."

Wow! That makes the experience almost seem cruel. Yet it brings to light the cruelty of so many of the life experiences we have had. It brings to light the cruelty of a world devastated by sin. Perhaps it makes us understand why we see ourselves the way we do. Maybe it helps us see the effects of our life experiences that leave us feeling like we are on top of the wave one minute only to be thrown to the ocean floor the next. In this we see the truth of C. S. Lewis's words when he said, "Experience: That most brutal of teachers."

The good news, and truth #4, is that Jesus always has the final word in our story, not our experience. The disciples are not identified as the, "men who struggled with the storm." They are identified as disciples of Christ. They aren't remembered because of their struggle; they are remembered because of the victory they found in Jesus. If we were to select a few words to define Peter, looking at his whole life story, we could select words like "apostle," "bold," "courageous," "repentant," "leader," and "founder of Jesus' church." Sure, we would acknowledge his mistakes and failures, but they wouldn't define him because we know the rest of the story.

How about you? What three words do you believe define your identity?

1. _____

2. _____

3. _____

If you are in Christ, He is your identity.

> You are not identified by your sin. You are identified by the righteousness of Christ.

> You are not identified as an adulterer. You are identified as the faithful bride of Jesus.

You are not identified as sexually promiscuous. You are identified as pure and spotless.

You are not identified as the one who was scarred by rape. You are identified as the one who is healed through faith.

You are not identified as the one who was abused and molested. You are identified as the one who is restored.

You are not identified as the one who was a slave to alcohol and drugs. You are identified as the one who is set free by grace.

Now evaluate the three words you selected to see if they point to a God-based identity or an experience-based identity. Write God-based or experience-based beside them.

Jesus has the final word. His final word is not one of condemnation to hold you back but a word of affirmation to propel you forward to your next step. And your next step with Christ is the first letter in the first word of a better story for your life.

We can't move on from this section of scripture without noting something in this text. The story continued so that others could be healed. There were others who needed a better story. There were other stories to be written. This is a huge part of our story because our story will always include the continuation of God's story. It is the gospel story that is still being written. Your story is one of the stories God needs to make His story complete.

The point of this chapter is to encourage you that God is writing a better story. He has a better story for you. As we continue to walk through this journey together, remember,

1. Jesus knows where you are.
2. Jesus is never as far as you think.
3. Jesus always gets us to the other side.
4. Jesus always has the final word in our stories.

CHAPTER 6

——◆——

THE BIG T TRUTH

Every word in the Bible was written to point us to Jesus. The account of Joseph's life is no different. In fact, the scriptures telling of the events of Joseph's life and his response to those events foreshadow the life and purpose of Jesus as clearly as any other in the Bible.

Just consider these commonalities.

- Joseph went into a foreign land so that he could ultimately save his people. So did Jesus.
- Joseph was rejected by his own people. So was Jesus.
- Joseph was highly favored by his father. So was Jesus.
- Joseph gave grace rather than the judgment that was deserved. So did Jesus.
- Joseph was sold into slavery for twenty pieces of silver. Jesus was sold for thirty.
- Joseph was stripped of his special robe. So was Jesus.
- Joseph was punished unjustly so others could have life. So was Jesus.

- Joseph faced false accusations. So did Jesus.
- Joseph's identity in God enabled him to fulfill his purpose. So did Jesus'. (Source Unknown)

I'm sure we could come up with even more similarities between Joseph and Jesus. Those are just a few to help you see how their lives paralleled in many ways. Obviously, Jesus was the perfection of humanity, and no other person lived the life He did. Joseph, like every person, existed to point people to Christ, and he fulfilled that purpose well. In fact, his story paints a vivid picture of the gospel story. In Genesis chapters 42 and 43, we see the power of God's grace as well as how our guilt and troubled hearts hinder us from receiving it and living out of it.

Before we get into the text, I want to set it up for you. At this point in Joseph's life, he is ruling over Egypt as Pharaoh's right-hand man. The dreams he interpreted for Pharaoh have come true, and there is a great famine in the land. Because of the wisdom given to Joseph by God, the Egyptians stored grain throughout the seven abundant years and now had plenty to sustain them through the seven years of famine. As people found out there was grain in Egypt, they came from all directions with cash in hand. Those who came in search of food included Joseph's brothers. I told you this is the making of a great reality television show!

Joseph was in charge of grain distribution, so the brothers' search for food brought them face to face with the one they sold into slavery twenty years earlier. Joseph recognized them, but they were unable to recognize him. Joseph accused his brothers of being spies and spoke to them through an interpreter in order to keep his identity hidden from them. He told them they must leave one of the brothers with him while they carried grain back to their starving families. Joseph promised to release the captive brother if they returned with

Benjamin, the youngest sibling. This conversation picks up with verse 18.

> On the third day, Joseph said to them, "Do this and you will live, for I fear God: If you are honest men, let one of your brothers stay here in prison, while the rest of you go and take grain back for your starving households. But you must bring your youngest brother to me, so that your words may be verified and that you may not die." This they proceeded to do.
>
> They said to one another, "Surely we are being punished because of our brother. We saw how distressed he was when he pleaded with us for his life, but we would not listen; that's why this distress has come on us."
>
> Reuben replied, "Didn't I tell you not to sin against the boy? But you wouldn't listen! Now we must give an accounting for his blood." They did not realize that Joseph could understand them, since he was using an interpreter.
>
> He turned away from them and began to weep, but then came back and spoke to them again. He had Simeon taken from them and bound before their eyes.
>
> Joseph gave orders to fill their bags with grain, to put each man's silver back in his sack, and to give them provisions for their journey. After this was done for them, they loaded their grain on their donkeys and left.

At the place where they stopped for the night one of them opened his sack to get feed for his donkey, and he saw his silver in the mouth of his sack. "My silver has been returned," he said to his brothers. "Here it is in my sack."

Their hearts sank and they turned to each other trembling and said, "What is this that God has done to us?"

Once the brothers reached their home, they had another horrifying discovery.

As they were emptying their sacks, there in each man's sack was his pouch of silver! When they and their father saw the money pouches, they were frightened.

Things went from bad to worse. It was bad enough that one of the brothers found the money he had given for grain in his sack, but now all of them had returned with their money. In their minds, this was a death sentence. If they remained in Canaan, they would starve to death. If they returned to Egypt, they would be imprisoned or killed because of their perceived theft.

After waiting awhile, it became clear that, while returning to Egypt with Benjamin meant possible death or imprisonment, staying in Canaan was certain death. Reluctantly, Jacob allowed the brothers to take Benjamin and return to Egypt.

Let's step away from Joseph's brothers' story for a moment to think about our own. I'm sure we've all heard stories that were told as the truth but actually weren't. We typically call that a lie. I would be willing to bet that at some point in our lives, we believed a story that wasn't true. In other words, we believed a lie.

For example, when I was about seven years old, my dad solemnly called me into his bedroom, where he proceeded to open his dresser drawer and tell me, "Son, I have a secret that I want to tell you, but you can't tell anyone else. Okay?" Of course I replied, "Okay!" He reached into the drawer and pulled out a silver .38 pistol cartridge and, with the same look of seriousness, said, "Son, I used to be the Lone Ranger!"

My jaw dropped! You have to understand that when I was seven, the Lone Ranger was being replayed every day. I was into the Lone Ranger way before he got lost in Johnny Depp's shadow. This was the greatest news I had ever heard. My dad was the Lone Ranger. Yes!

Even though he told me not to tell anyone, I went out and told *everyone*. How could you keep that a secret? When I found out it wasn't true, I was crushed.

While that story was really harmless, and I really wasn't all that crushed, we all have stories in our lives that have hurt us. Whether or not we realize it, each of us have believed stories that tell us things that may or may not be true about ourselves. Those stories are told to us through experiences we have in our lives. So far we've looked at how the events of our lives, cultures, and our primary caregivers all shape how we see ourselves. While some experiences may tell us the truth about our character, value, and worth, many do not.

Think about all the people in scripture who would have never made a difference in the world if they believed the stories their experiences told them. Joseph would have wasted away in Pharaoh's prison and never interpreted the baker's and cupbearer's dreams. He would have never been put in a position to save his people. Moses would have never gone to Pharaoh because he didn't believe he could speak well enough. Gideon would have never gotten out of the wine press he was hiding in to go fight the Midianites. David would have always shepherded sheep rather than shepherding God's people. Isaiah would have always seen himself as unclean rather than going and proclaiming God's Word to His people and pointing us to Jesus through his prophecy. Matthew would have died in his guilt and shame as a tax collector, having never penned the first gospel account that bears his name. Paul would have drowned in the guilt of murder rather than becoming the greatest missionary the world has ever seen. God had a better story for these Bible heroes than what their experiences told them. God has a better story than what your experiences have told you.

The world's system tells us that we are defined by our experiential stories. We are the sum total of what we've done, what we are doing, what we will do, and what's been done to us. We have different labels put on us by the media, our cultures, our friends, and our families. We are labeled as divorced, widowed, addicted, promiscuous, homosexual, unforgiving, and so on. There is no end to the list of labels we are given. Is there any wonder we live with identity crises when we are constantly labeled by the influences around us?

Getting back to Joseph's brothers, what labels did the brothers wear? Were they "unloved," "betrayers," "worthless"? The label that horrified the brothers the most was that of "guilty"! The label was true, but Joseph had forgiven the debt. Granted, there are a lot of variables in play in this story, but at the core of the brothers' issues was their mistreatment of Joseph. Look back again at Genesis chapter 42.

> They said to one another, "Surely we are being
> punished because of our brother. We saw how
> distressed he was when he pleaded with us for his

life, but we would not listen; that's why this distress
has come on us."

Reuben replied, "Didn't I tell you not to sin against
the boy? But you wouldn't listen! Now we must give
an accounting for his blood."

In their hearts, they knew they deserved to be punished for their
heinous crime. Something that happened twenty years earlier still
haunted them, keeping the brothers from being able to receive what
Joseph was freely giving them. It was a barrier between them.

I believe most of us are the same way. Our experiences have told us
stories about ourselves that we believed. What we have concluded
about ourselves from those experiences becomes a barrier to receiving
the treasure that God wants to pour into our hearts and lives.

It makes me think of putting plastic wrap over the top of a cup and
then trying to pour water into it. As Christians, it is often a barrier
caused by our guilty and troubled hearts that prevents us from
receiving love from God or anyone else. Yet, if we are in Christ, the
barrier does not exist. But we can't imagine that Jesus understands
our plight, much less forgives our trespasses. Read verse 23 again.

They did not realize that Joseph could understand
them, since he was using an interpreter.

Don't miss this! There was a perceived communication gap between
Joseph and his brothers that didn't actually exist. This is how most
of us live in relationship with Jesus. We simply cannot accept that,
in our imperfection, He loves us perfectly. Because of this perceived
barrier, we are unable to receive the treasure of God's grace that He
desires to pour into our hearts.

In the Old Testament temple worship, a veil separated all the other areas of the temple from what is called the Holy of Holies. The veil was a boundary set by God that no one was allowed to enter into because of their sins. Once a year, the high priest went into the Holy of Holies to make sacrifices for the people's sins. For the people of God, the veil represented the separation from God created by their sins. When Jesus died on the cross, we are told that the veil in the temple was literally and physically, "torn in two from top to bottom" (Matthew 27:51). This was a huge observation because it meant that the wall erected between us and God, because of sin, had been destroyed by Jesus's sacrificial death.

There is no longer anything separating those who are in Christ from their heavenly Father. Paul emphatically stresses this point in Romans chapter 8.

> For I am convinced that neither death nor life, neither angels nor demons, neither the present nor the future, nor any powers, neither height nor depth, nor anything else in all creation, will be able to separate us from the love of God that is in Christ Jesus our Lord.

What can separate those who are in Christ from His love? Nothing! The fact that the barrier no longer exists—and is only a barrier erected in our minds—is what I find most heartbreaking for those of us who are in Christ.

Let this sink in. The veil has been torn once and for all. God doesn't zip it back together when we are "bad" and unzip it when we are "good." It is forever destroyed for those who are in Christ. It means that we are eternally able to go into God's presence, not because of who we are, but because of who we are in Christ. We are able to go into His presence, not because of what we've done, but because of what Jesus has done for us. This means no matter what you were before Christ, you are that no more. No matter who you were before Christ, you are that person no more. You have become a new creation; the old is gone and the new has come (2 Corinthians 5:17). Understand this; we go boldly before God's throne to receive grace and mercy to help us live like Christ, not to be reminded of our sins (Hebrews 4:16). Labels, other than that of "in Christ," can no longer stick to you. This is your new identity.

I want to be careful with the simplicity of this, but I don't want to overcomplicate it either. I want to be clear that I'm not making light of your experiences or telling you they aren't true. I would never tell you that you should "just get over it." That's not the point. Those experiences are true. They really did happen. They really do write a truth upon our hearts, and we draw real conclusions from them. But there is a truth that is greater than your experiences. There is a truth that is greater than your troubled heart and the conclusions you've drawn about yourself from those experiences. This truth is the truth of God's Word and the gospel story. This is where we find a true and better story for our lives.

The objection, which comes from religious fear, is that when people are told they are no longer sinners and are completely free from sin will sin more. Paul addressed this issue in Romans 6:1–4.

> What shall we say, then? Shall we go on sinning so that grace may increase? By no means! We are those who have died to sin; how can we live in it any longer? Or don't you know that all of us who were baptized into Christ Jesus were baptized into his death? We were therefore buried with him through baptism into death in order that, just as Christ was raised from the dead through the glory of the Father, we too may live a new life.

Paul is saying that in Christ, you are free to live a new life because the old, sinful life is dead. Through our faith in Christ, our old life has been nailed to the cross with Jesus and, like Jesus, we have been raised to new life. If the old life is dead, it means it is gone, out of the picture, and unable to hold us back anymore. As Christians, we work so hard to try and raise the old, dead life when we should just quit dragging it along, cut the ties, and walk in the freedom of new life.

Here's the reality that we must accept as Christians. We don't become more like Jesus because of our guilt. We become more like Jesus because of grace.

If guilt could remake us into the image of God, the old covenant law would have sufficed. Until we begin to see ourselves as Jesus sees us, we will never be able to live as Jesus lived. We can even come to faith in Christ, be given a new heart at conversion, be filled with the Holy Spirit, and begin to have new desires but still find it impossible to do the things we desire to do. What should we do? Try harder? Work harder? That's exactly what Joseph's brothers did. This is the account of what happened when Jacob finally allowed them to return to Egypt to purchase more grain.

> Then their father Israel said to them, "If it must be, then do this: Put some of the best products of the land in your bags and take them down to the man as a gift—a little balm and a little honey, some spices and myrrh, some pistachio nuts and almonds. Take double the amount of silver with you, for you must return the silver that was put back into the mouths of your sacks. Perhaps it was a mistake. Take your brother also and go back to the man at once. And may God Almighty grant you mercy before the man so that he will let your other brother

and Benjamin come back with you. As for me, if I
am bereaved, I am bereaved."

So the men took the gifts and double the amount
of silver, and Benjamin also. They hurried down to
Egypt and presented themselves to Joseph.

What did the brothers do? They did a little more than they did last
time. They worked a little harder to gain Joseph's favor. They gave
a little more to appease his anger. They petitioned with all of their
gifts to make themselves acceptable to the "lord of the land." They
doubled-down and tried harder to please Joseph.

How often do we do the same thing? We think, *I'll just work a little
harder.* We tell ourselves, "When I get my stuff together, I'll come
to God." Jesus didn't come for those who were well and had it all
together. He came for the sick and those hanging on by a thread. He
came to make the sinner a saint and the brokenhearted whole. He
came to make the wounded well and set the captive free.

Doing more didn't work for Joseph's brothers. Joseph had no need of
anything they had. What Joseph wanted was simply to be reconciled
to them. God is the same way. He has no need of our superficial
auditions and performances. He simply wants the reconciliation
of Himself and His creation. That happens through the grace He
gives us through Jesus. Understand, grace is God's unmerited, or
undeserved, favor. If His favor could be earned through what you
do, grace would cease to be grace.

It is through an initial reception of grace through faith in Jesus that we
are saved. It is through continually receiving grace through Jesus that
our minds are renewed to see our new identities. Growing into our
identities in Christ is the process of sanctification. "Sanctification"
is a word that, in "Christianese," means to become more like Jesus.

All Christians go through this process. Basically, sanctification is us growing into the identities God has already given us through Jesus. At salvation, our hearts are made new, and we begin a new journey with a new life. But our minds are still being renewed.

The apostle Paul tells us in Romans 12:2, "Do not be conformed any longer to the pattern of this world, but be transformed by the renewing of your mind." The mind is the control center for our thoughts and actions. As we begin to see ourselves according to the truth of God's Word and according to the Spirit of Christ inside us, our minds and hearts are united and come into agreement within our new life. It is the Word of Christ that tells us who we are, and it is the Spirit of Christ that confirms who we are as He cries out from the core of our being, "Abba, Father" (Galatians 4:6).

When we begin to see ourselves as having new natures, we begin to live and act according to that nature. But you cannot live consistently privately and publicly as Christ until you see yourself as Christ does. On the flip side, you cannot continue to live contrary to Christ when you see yourself as Christ does. Why? It's no longer according to your nature, or who you really are. A dog doesn't act like a goldfish; it's not in a dog's nature to do so. You will live according to the way you believe you are. If you want to glorify God, it doesn't come from trying harder. It comes from receiving His love, the gospel truth of who you are in Christ, and living out of that love.

So what are we to do? Really? How does this work out practically in my life? It begins by receiving the truth of Jesus (the "Big T") as your identity and rejecting your experiential truth (the "little t") as having the power to define you. It is basically letting Jesus—rather than your experience—have the final word in your life. If you are in Christ, He tells you who you are, not you or anyone else. Quit arguing with God! You'll lose every time.

Here's an illustration that I hope will help you see how we do this. One of my wife's favorite games to play is the card game Spades. In this game, four people form two teams, and each player is dealt thirteen cards. The players look at their cards and bid on how many "tricks," or rounds, they think they can win. Each round is won by having the highest card of the suit that is played. (Ace is high; two is low.) If someone does not have the suit being played, he or she may play a spade. The spade trumps, or beats, any card other than a higher spade. That is a really bad description of the game of Spades but hopefully enough information to make my point. There is one card that can be played that no other card is able to beat: the ace of spades. The ace of spades trumps every other card. In no situation or circumstance does any card beat the ace of spades. Naturally, this is the card you want to be dealt.

I'm not telling you about my wife's love of a card game or the power of the ace of spades just to fill up a page. I'm giving you this information to help you see the power of having something in your life that trumps everything else. We need an ace of spades in our lives. We need something that has the power to trump everything else, no matter what the situation, circumstance, or experience. If we are to live with an accurate identity and in the fullness of life God desires for us, that something is the Bible, God's Word.

We use anchors to keep boats steady through wind and storms. In the same way, God's Word anchors our lives in the storms of experience that try to determine our identities. Much like the relentless pounding of the ocean's waves erodes the seashore, the thousands of experiences we have each day pound at our hearts, relentlessly trying to erode any sense of a true identity. We, in and of ourselves, are powerless against the forces of our experiences, and our identities will be established by our experiences. However, if we play our trump card, and play it consistently, we establish identities that set us free from our experiential truths.

Maybe the defining card in your life has been addiction, and the story it has written tells you that you will never be able to break free from this bondage. That card is trumped by the truth that in all things we are more than conquerors through Jesus who loves us. Is the card that defines you one of broken relationships that riddle you with guilt and condemnation? That card is trumped by the truth that there is no condemnation for those who are in Christ (Romans 8:1).

Perhaps the card that has defined your life has been tragedy that has caused crippling emotional pain, and you simply don't believe you will ever be able to experience joy again. That card is trumped by the truth that our God is a God of comfort and compassion who comforts us in all our troubles so that we can comfort others with the comfort we've received from Him. Not only does He have a better story for you, He desires for your story to impact the stories of others. Life is not over.

Maybe your life has been paralyzed by a card of fear. That card is trumped by the truth that when I seek the Lord, He will answer me; He delivers me from all my fears (Psalm 34:4). He did not give me a spirit of fear but of power and love and a sound mind (2 Timothy 1:7). Whenever those lying cards of experience come up and attempt to create your story and redefine your identity, trump them with the truth of God's Word.

Watch how this plays out in our thought processes and how it begins to renew our minds. We'll use our "How Did I Get Here?" story to see this practically. As you read through your story, evaluate each sentence or thought as true or false. If the statement is true according to God's truth about you, write "True," with a capital T, beside that statement. If it is not true according to God's Word, write, "Bull" beside it. "Bull" can stand for whatever you want it to as long as it is strong enough to reinforce how untrue the statement is. For our more-sanctified folks, it may stand for "bull"oney. Okay, I realize that's not how you spell it, but work with me here. For those who aren't quite as sanctified, or are pretty hardheaded like me, you can use "Bull" to represent whatever reinforces the fact that the statement is completely untrue according to God's Word about you.

Here's part of my "How Did I Get Here?" which I shared in chapter 2, to help you get started.

> I was very strong in faith when we moved into full-time ministry. (True) We saw God do amazing things that got us there, like our business selling in a month. (True) The stresses of ministry were definitely felt then, but my faith was strong, and I really trusted in God's promises. (True)
>
> I think the first time I really questioned anything was when we left my position as a youth pastor at one church and moved to another as the associate pastor. (True) I was confident because I was so sure I "heard God" tell us to go. (True) When it went south so quickly and there was so much hurt, I began to wonder if I had made a mistake. (Bull) Did I miss God's leading? (Bull) I began to seriously doubt myself. (True)
>
> It seemed that everything I was confident in was disintegrating. (Bull) On my thirty-third birthday I found myself in a cabin, miles from nowhere, with a wife and two kids, no job, and a "pastor" with no ministry. (True) It was during that time at the cabin that I began to feel great confirmation of my calling as a pastor and where I felt God gave me a vision for Connection Church. (True) I felt very sure about

my calling but was very unsettled about the church. On one hand, I felt that the Lord was leading us, but in the back of my mind was the question, "Are you messing up again?" (Bull), with no clear indication I had "messed up" before. Even after God began to do amazing things, I still worried that I had done the wrong thing. (Bull) Even a very bad thing (by starting the church). (Double Bull) I took a lot of criticism from people in town and at our old church. It hurt deeply and reinforced that what I had done was wrong, and I was wrong. (Bull, Bull, Bull!)

We kept pushing through it all, but it took a very heavy toll. I was wiped out before we started, and the physical, emotional, and spiritual stress of starting a church, working a full-time job, and finishing my master's didn't refuel my tank and only made things worse. (True)

After a couple of years, I came under a new type of criticism. It was criticism from within the church, not from the outside. (True) I was accused of begin a heretic. (Bull) I was told I preached works-based salvation. (Bull) I was given a book called *The Gospel* because, "I didn't preach the real gospel." (Bull) And I was told I preached a "man-centered gospel" and not a "God-centered gospel." (Bull) I think, as I reflect on it, that was the beginning of my crisis of faith because everything I believed had been challenged. (True) I had attended churches that had some theological errors, but what church or denomination doesn't? I began to struggle with whether or not I was in error and whether or not I was wrong again and, even worse, leading people astray. (Bull × 10^{15}!)

You can see that as I began to move away from factual information to the thoughts and emotions the facts caused, I began to have a lot more Bull than Truth! I was in a full-blown identity crisis that spiraled me into depression and affected every relationship in my life, including my relationship with God. Now you go through your own "How Did I Get Here?" story. Separate the factual information from the thoughts and emotions, and see how many lies you've believed about yourself.

I hope you are beginning to sense how freeing it could be to live in the truth, being only defined by God's Word. It is only in the truth that you can find an accurate identity for yourself. The truth ("Big T") trumps our experiential truth ("Little t") and sets us free as new creations in Christ.

In chapter 43 of Genesis, Joseph's brothers return to Egypt with Benjamin. They've brought their "double-portions" to try and appease Joseph and evade punishment. Then they begin to explain to Joseph's servant what happened.

> So the men took the gifts and double the amount of silver, and Benjamin also. They hurried down to Egypt and presented themselves to Joseph. When Joseph saw Benjamin with them, he said to the steward of his house, "Take these men to my house, slaughter an animal and prepare a meal; they are to eat with me at noon."
>
> The man did as Joseph told him and took the men to Joseph's house. Now the men were frightened when they were taken to his house. They thought,

"We were brought here because of the silver that was put back into our sacks the first time. He wants to attack us and overpower us and seize us as slaves and take our donkeys."

So they went up to Joseph's steward and spoke to him at the entrance to the house. "We beg your pardon, our lord," they said, "we came down here the first time to buy food. But at the place where we stopped for the night we opened our sacks and each of us found his silver—the exact weight—in the mouth of his sack. So we have brought it back with us. We have also brought additional silver with us to buy food. We don't know who put our silver in our sacks."

"It's all right," he said. "Don't be afraid. Your God, the God of your father, has given you treasure in your sacks; I received your silver." Then he brought Simeon out to them.

The steward took the men into Joseph's house, gave them water to wash their feet and provided fodder for their donkeys. They prepared their gifts for Joseph's arrival at noon, because they had heard that they were to eat there.

Here we see another link, or foreshadowing, of Jesus and Joseph. The gifts Joseph gave to the men are said to have been given by God. God, working through Joseph, had put great treasure in the brothers' sacks even though their guilty consciences and troubled hearts prevented them from receiving it. Just as God gave the brothers great treasure in grain and silver, He has given us a great treasure in Jesus. Just as Joseph planted the treasure in the brothers' sacks, God has planted the truth of Jesus within our hearts. How much better off would we be if we just lived out of the treasure He has given us? How much freer would we be to live for God and enjoy Him forever? If we live with the light of God's truth shining in our hearts, revealing our identities in Christ, we will find that John 8:32 is true.

Then you will know the truth, and the truth will set you free." When I was in Colorado at the Blessing Ranch, I wrote a letter. It wasn't an ordinary letter; God inspired it. It wasn't about my feelings and emotions; it was full of His truth and treasure in my life. It came from scripture, God's letter written to us. It has become the greatest tool in my toolbox as I build an accurate identity in Christ. This is the letter that God gave me.

> Dear Brandon,
>
> Trust in the truth and not what your experience says. (Trust in the Lord with all your heart and lean not on your own understanding; in all your ways submit to him, and he will make your paths straight. [Proverbs 3:5, 6].) I have called you to preach My gospel and lead My church. (Although I am less than the least of all the Lord's people, this grace was given me: to preach to the Gentiles the boundless riches of Christ, and to make plain to everyone the administration of this mystery, which for ages past was kept hidden in God, who created all things. His intent was that now, through the church, the manifold wisdom of God should be made known to the rulers and authorities in the heavenly realms, according to his eternal purpose that he accomplished in Christ Jesus our Lord [Ephesians 3:8–11].) You are competent and able because I have created, equipped, and purposed you for this task. (Now to each one the manifestation of the Spirit is

given for the common good [1 Corinthians 12:7];
Such confidence we have through Christ before
God. Not that we are competent in ourselves to
claim anything for ourselves, but our competence
comes from God. He has made us competent as
ministers of a new covenant—not of the letter
but of the Spirit; for the letter kills, but the Spirit
gives life [2 Corinthians 3:4–6].) I want you to see
yourself as I see you. I delight in you and there is
no condemnation for you. (Therefore, there is now
no condemnation for those who are in Christ Jesus
[Romans 8:1]; The Lord your God is with you, the
Mighty Warrior who saves. He will take great delight
in you; in his love he will no longer rebuke you, but
will rejoice over you with singing [Zephaniah 3:17];
My dear children, let's not just talk about love; let's
practice real love. This is the only way we'll know
we're living truly, living in God's reality. It's also the
way to shut down debilitating self-criticism, even
when there is something to it. For God is greater
than our worried hearts and knows more about us
than we do ourselves [1 John 3:16–18 MSG].) You
are my child and I love you. (Because you are his
sons, God sent the Spirit of his Son into our hearts,
the Spirit who calls out, "*Abba*, Father." So you
are no longer a slave, but God's child; and since
you are his child, God has made you also an heir
[Galatians 4:6–7]; This is how God showed his
love among us: He sent his one and only Son into
the world that we might live through him. This is
love: not that we loved God, but that he loved us
and sent his Son as an atoning sacrifice for our sins
[1 John 4:9, 10].) No matter what anyone else says,
you are okay because I have said you are okay. (But

now apart from the law the righteousness of God has been made known, to which the Law and the Prophets testify. This righteousness is given through faith in Jesus Christ to all who believe. There is no difference between Jew and Gentile, for all have sinned and fall short of the glory of God, and all are justified freely by his grace through the redemption that came by Christ Jesus. God presented Christ as a sacrifice of atonement, through the shedding of his blood—to be received by faith. He did this to demonstrate his righteousness, because in his forbearance he had left the sins committed beforehand unpunished— he did it to demonstrate his righteousness at the present time, so as to be just and the one who justifies those who have faith in Jesus [Romans 3:21–26].) Now, be strong and courageous, standing firm on these truths. ("Be strong and courageous, because you will lead these people to inherit the land I swore to their ancestors to give them. Be strong and very courageous. Be careful to obey all the law my servant Moses gave you; do not turn from it to the right or to the left, that you may be successful wherever you go. Keep this Book of the Law always on your lips; meditate on it day and night, so that you may be careful to do everything written in it. Then you will be prosperous and successful. Have I not commanded you? Be strong and courageous. Do not be afraid; do not be discouraged, for the Lord your God will be with you wherever you go" [Joshua 1:6–9].) Live out of grace and love by both giving it and receiving it. (But if anyone obeys his word, love for God is truly made complete in them. This is how we know we are in him: Whoever claims to live in him must live as Jesus did [1 John 2:5, 6; Then Peter said, "Silver or gold I do not have, but what I do have I give you. In the name of Jesus Christ of Nazareth, walk" [Acts 3:6]; Finally, be strong in the Lord and in his mighty power. Put on the full armor of God, so that you can take your stand against the devil's schemes. For our struggle is not against flesh and blood, but against the rulers, against the authorities, against the powers of this dark world and against the spiritual forces of evil in the heavenly realms. Therefore, put on the full armor of God, so that when the day of evil comes, you may be able to stand your ground, and after you have done everything, to stand. Stand firm then, with the belt of truth buckled around your waist, with the breastplate of righteousness in place, and with your feet fitted with the readiness that comes from the gospel of peace. In addition to all this, take up the shield of faith, with which you can extinguish all the flaming arrows of the evil one. Take the helmet of salvation and the sword of the Spirit, which is the word of God. And pray in the Spirit on all occasions with all kinds of prayers and requests. With this in mind, be alert and always keep on praying for all the Lord's people [Ephesians 6:10–18].) Preach boldly and lead courageously because I am in this with you, and you will finish this race well! (Being confident of this, that he who began a good work in you will carry it on to completion until the day of Christ Jesus [Philippians 1:6]; Not that I have already obtained all this, or have already arrived at my goal, but I press on to take hold of that for which Christ Jesus took hold of me. Brothers and sisters, I do not consider myself yet to have taken hold of it.

But one thing I do: Forgetting what is behind and straining toward what is ahead, I press on toward the goal to win the prize for which God has called me heavenward in Christ Jesus [Philippians 3:12–14]; I have fought the good fight, I have finished the race, I have kept the faith [2 Timothy 4:7]; fixing our eyes on Jesus, the author and perfecter of our faith. For the joy set before him he endured the cross, scorning its shame, and sat down at the right hand of the throne of God. Consider him who endured such opposition from sinners, so that you will not grow weary and lose heart [Hebrews 12:2, 3].) You are my son with whom I am well pleased. (And a voice from heaven said, "This is my Son, whom I love; with him I am well pleased" [Matthew 3:17]; For you died, and your life is now hidden with Christ in God [Colossians 3:3]; God made him who had no sin to be sin for us, so that in him we might become the righteousness of God [2 Corinthians 5:21]; So in Christ Jesus you are all children of God through faith, for all of you who were baptized into Christ have clothed yourselves with Christ [Galatians 3:26, 27].) Rely on and live in my love. (And so we know and rely on the love God has for us. God is love. Whoever lives in love lives in God, and God in them [1 John 4:16].)

God

You have written your "How Did I Get Here?" It was full of some truths, some half-truths, and many lies. Now we need to write a true story. It is God's message to you. God's truth is the greatest treasure we have, and we must receive this treasure and receive it often if we are to live freely and in a way that glorifies Him. Here are some of the treasures God has given us. Use them to write a letter from God to you from His Word. Use these scriptures to get you started, but don't be limited to them. Search God's Word for His message to you. His Word is living and active (Hebrews 4:12). Let it speak a better story into your life.

This letter is important. It will become a tool in your toolbox as you build an identity that is accurate in Christ. Get started!

In Christ

- I am a new creation.
  - o   2 Corinthians 5:17

- I can trust God to continue to work in me.
  - o   Philippians 1:6

- I am God's handiwork.
  - o   Ephesians 2:10

- I am good enough because of the work of Christ.
  - o   Titus 3:5

- I have peace with God.
  - o   Romans 5:1–2

- I am shown love through the work on the cross.
  - o   Romans 5:6–8

- I am forgiven.
  - o   1 John 1:9

- God wants to use me.
  - o   1 Timothy 1:12–14

- God favors me.
  - o 1 Corinthians 15:10

- I have the gift of salvation.
  - o Ephesians 2:8

- I have everything I need.
  - o 2 Peter 1:3

- I am equipped.
  - o 1 Corinthians 1:5

- I am gifted.
  - o 1 Corinthians 1:7

- I am strong.
  - o 2 Corinthians 12:9

- I can do anything.
  - o Philippians 4:13

- I have a spirit of power, love, and self-control.
  - o 2 Timothy 1:7

- I have no fear.
  - o Isaiah 41:10

- I have a future.
  - o Jeremiah 29:11

- I do not have to worry.
  - o Matthew 6:25–27

- I do not have to be afraid.
  - o Joshua 1:9

- I am treasured.
  - o Deuteronomy 14:2

- I am chosen.
  - o Isaiah 41:9

- I am called out of darkness.
  - o 1 Peter 2:9

- I am accepted.
  - o Psalm 94:14

- I am wonderfully made.
  - o Psalm 139:13–14

- I am child of God.
  - o 1 John 3:1

- I am loved.
  - o 1 John 4:10

  - o Romans 5:8

- Nothing can separate me from the love of God.
  - o Romans 8:38–39

- God is bigger than my condemnation.
  - o 1 John 3:19–20

- I have overcome the world.
  - o 1 John 5:4–5

- I am free.
  - o Galatians 5:1

- I am gifted, equipped, and competent.
  o 2 Corinthians 3:4–6

- I am free from sin and condemnation.
  o Romans 8:1

- I have an eternal purpose.
  o Colossians 3:2

CHAPTER 7

BATTLE ON

As a child, I loved to play anything that was outdoors and involved a ball. It didn't matter if it was kickball, baseball, football, or any other sport that ended in "ball." I was in! In one of our "ball" games, we would occasionally end up in a disagreement over a play. The ball would hit a power line, or some other irresolvable situation would take place, and we would have to resort to using a term that solved all unsolvable situations: "do-over."

A do-over seemed to fix everything! It was the mediator of hostile kids, competing for playground supremacy. Simple, yet profound, the do-over worked miracles and saved games that seemed to be beyond saving. It means exactly what it sounds like. Do that play, that pitch, that kick, over again. Do-over!

I bet that for many of us, the thought of a do-over is nice. However, the do-over we would like carries more weight than playground pride. I bet we would like to have a do-over in life. We'd love to get another chance at all of it, or at least a part of it. The do-over would be used to eliminate the "them," "they," or "it" we talked about in earlier chapters. In removing those encounters, we would remove the sore spots they created, and life would be whole. I hope by now you see that you can indeed heal the sore spots even though a do-over is not possible.

I don't think we would be alone in our desire for a do-over. I feel pretty confident that every person who's ever existed has had that thought at some point in time, including our original parents, Adam and Eve. They were the first people that God formed, fashioned, and breathed life into, and they were placed in paradise with only one commandment: "You are free to eat from any tree in the garden; but you must not eat from the tree of the knowledge of good and evil, for when you eat of it you will surely die" (Genesis 3:1).

One command. That's all. Don't eat the fruit from that tree, and you can live in paradise forever! Here are my questions to what followed next.

1. Can we get a do-over?
2. How do you muddle that up?
3. How could you be surrounded by trees with fruit and have to eat the fruit from the only tree God said not to eat from?

Answer to that last one: the same way we are surrounded by God's blessings that bring life and still choose those things that bring death.

Granted, it seems a lot more complicated for us than it was for Adam and Eve. There are so many more choices and influences in our lives. While it is true that there are more influences around us, their power to derail us is fueled by the same temptation that fatally wounded the first man and woman. This temptation was a challenge to their identities. I really want you to realize that our identities are not an issue; it is *the* issue. Satan has one pitch to throw, and it is designed to move your eyes from your identity in Christ to identity in other things so that you will worship something or someone else.

I mentioned my lackluster collegiate baseball career earlier. One of the many reasons that it was less than spectacular was because I could not hit an inside fastball. There are a lot of technical reasons why I wasn't able to hit it, but for this illustration, just understand that if a guy was throwing relatively hard, and I didn't know what was coming, I simply couldn't get my bat to the ball in time. It was a pitch that, once the pitcher realized it, was impossible for me to hit. The only way I could hit it was if I knew what was coming.

Here's the bad news. Satan's identity pitch is a really good pitch. Here's the good news. Once we identify it, realize it's coming, and learn how to hit it, he has nothing else to throw at us. It's his only weapon. He just disguises it in different ways. Until we learn to recognize his pitch early, we are swinging at pitches that we cannot hit. You could say we are fighting a losing battle even though, as Christians, we have won the war.

Let's look at how Satan pitched an identity crisis into the lives of Adam and Eve. We know from Genesis chapter 1 that God made Adam in His image. He gave Adam everything he needed for a fruitful and joyful life. Part of "everything" included his wife, Eve, who was placed beside him to be a helpmate and a partner in life. As God's image bearers, they were able to accurately reflect God's glory throughout the earth.

Then Satan comes on the scene. He tempts them by challenging the very words that God told them. In doing so, Satan makes them think that somehow God is holding out on them. They begin to believe the lie that they can attain greater value and worth apart from God. In their distorted minds, they actually began to think a better identity than one that reflects the glory of God was possible. They began to covet and worship the fruit rather than the fruit-giver. Whenever we worship something other than God, we become an idol worshipper. I believe that Adam and Eve's greatest sin was not the sin of eating the fruit. I believe the greatest sin was the sin of idolatry that produced the fruit of disobedience.

Because of their disobedience, Adam and Eve could no longer remain in God's presence. Sin always separates us from God in one way or another. The Bible records the scene this way in Genesis chapter 3.

> The Lord God made garments of skin for Adam and his wife and clothed them. And the Lord God said, "The man has now become like one of us, knowing good and evil. He must not be allowed to reach out his hand and take also from the tree of life and eat, and live forever." So the Lord God banished him from the Garden of Eden to work the ground from which he had been taken. After he drove the man out, he placed on the east side of the Garden of Eden cherubim and a flaming sword flashing back and forth to guard the way to the tree of life.

God's grace and mercy are seen in His willingness to cover Adam's and Eve's newfound nakedness and their resulting shame by killing, or sacrificing, an animal to make fur coats for them. However, the sacrifice wasn't sufficient to take away the sins that separated them from Him. That sacrifice would not come until the Perfect Lamb of God, Jesus, was slain on a cross thousands of years later. So Adam and Eve were put out of the garden and separated from the perfect fellowship they had enjoyed with God. With this separation came a separation from their Image Bearer, in whose likeness they were created. With this separation and their own images now marred by sin, the only battle humanity has ever known exploded into an all-out war. It was a fight to recover a lost identity. We, as humanity, have been fighting this war ever since, and Satan has been throwing us his pitch of identity crisis with great success.

It was not until Jesus came into the world that we were able to see how humanity was intended to look. Only in Christ are we able to once again get a clear view of our intended image. Yet, with such a clear representation of who we are in Christ, we are still caught in a war of identity. Living in Christ and in our identities is not a fight; it is *the* fight. It is the conflict within us that, once resolved, finally brings peace to our troubled souls and life to our dry bones. However, we do not have peace and life without the fight. We must realize it will be a fight, but the prize we win is worthy of our greatest efforts. The question now becomes, "How do I fight?"

The Fight

I can honestly say it all happened so fast that it now seems like a blur. All I remember are flashes of light followed by moments of darkness. It was almost like painful strobe lights as his fist took turns hitting my eyes. I was only about eight or nine years old. He was about eleven or twelve, and what had been "trash" talking between kids turned really violent.

It happened as I was walking home from my friend's house. He only lived two houses down the street, but that was enough of a distance for the older kid to take opportunity to jump me and finish a childish argument that I thought was resolved the day before. I really never saw this attack coming, and I paid the price for it. One thing I can tell you for sure is I beat his fist to pieces with my face! Is that a victory in some small way? You're right; probably not.

I left the scene with swollen eyes from the beating and from tears. This story ends with my dad marching me down to the boy's house, knocking on the door, and telling his dad that if he ever saw the boy near me again, he was going to find him (the boy's dad) and "whip his hind end!" I really cleaned that up for this book! Yes, we were and probably still are rednecks, but you have to love a dad who will take up for you that way.

There are several things in this story that apply to our lives and that most Christians miss, don't know, or overlook. The first is that we don't realize we are in a fight. We continually get "jumped" by Satan's attacks on our identities in Christ, yet we accept it as, "This is just the way I am. I will always be this way." When we don't recognize the fight, we sacrifice the better story that God has for us on the altar of ignorance. We, as God's people, should not be caught off guard and certainly should not live in ignorance as God has revealed both His plan to give us life and Satan's plan to destroy us.

> The thief comes only to steal and kill and destroy;
> I have come that they may have life, and have it to
> the full. (John 10:10)

God's plan for life is life in Christ. Satan's plan to destroy life is to move our identities from Jesus to anything else, even if "anything" is a good thing. Not even things we call "good" are able to give us accurate identities.

The context of Jesus's saying in John 10:10 is within a parable of a shepherd and his sheep. The entire parable speaks to the fact that sheep, because they belong to the shepherd, know whose they are. The sheep identify with the shepherd and will follow no other voice but his. What results is a life of care and provision. The shepherd has a better story for the sheep than the sheep can write for themselves. Identifying ourselves as belonging to Jesus, the Good Shepherd, results in us following His voice and His words. Following His voice always leads us to life and a better story.

The Bible is clear about Satan's desire to destroy us.

> Be alert and of sober mind. Your enemy the devil
> prowls around like a roaring lion looking for
> someone to devour. (1 Peter 5:8)

In this text, we are told to be aware of the fight, and we see clearly Satan's desire not only to hurt us but also to completely devour us. The Greek word for "devour" means to "drink or swallow down." It tells us that he wants to completely consume us rather than us being consumed by Jesus. One way is death. The other is life.

We are in a fight! The stakes are high. It is a fight for our lives. Make it a fight, but fight wisely.

When I got pelted by my older adversary (Notice I always say "older." It makes the beating easier on my ego.), I had no clue how to fight. I was good at taking a beating, but I had no idea how to fight back. How to fight and win the battle of identity and ultimately the battle for life is another area that we, as Christians, often live in ignorance. If we are to live an abundant life and not just exist, we must learn how to fight. We must know how to stand. Paul sheds light on how we fight in 2 Corinthians 10.

> For though we live in the world, we do not wage
> war as the world does. The weapons we fight with
> are not the weapons of the world. On the contrary,
> they have divine power to demolish strongholds. We
> demolish arguments and every pretension that sets
> itself up against the knowledge of God, and we take
> captive every thought to make it obedient to Christ.

Even though we live in the world, we don't fight according to the world's system. We cannot overcome the world by winning in the system of the world. We, as the saying goes, are called to be in the world but not of it. We are called to operate within its boundaries but not be bound by how it operates. We operate, or live our lives, in Christ by establishing identities that are greater than the ones the world tries to put upon us. Understand that if you do not accept the identity Jesus gives you and establish His identity as your very own, the world will establish one for you.

Paul tells us we have been given weapons to use in our fights for identities. He assures us that the weapons we have been given by God have the power to get the job done. He also tells us that these weapons are effective for "demolishing strongholds."

Strongholds are ways of thinking. They affect the way we think about others, the world, and ourselves. They become firmly established in our minds. They are created by our experiences in the world and shape how we view everything, especially how we see ourselves in Christ. Our weapons are given to us by God to renew our minds and see our existence in this world very differently.

There is an old saying that goes, "You never bring a knife to a gunfight." Thankfully, I've never been in either. But it makes sense that we need the right weapons and armament if we are going to fight effectively. We know there really is an enemy who does not just seek to hinder our lives; he seeks to destroy our lives. We know his target is our identity in Christ. And we know his greatest weapons are accusation and condemnation. No wonder his alias is "the accuser of the brethren" (Revelation 12:10). The good news is that Jesus sits at the right hand of God and shoots those accusations down faster than Satan can send them up. Jesus is our intercessor and mediator. He speaks to the Father on our behalf and intercepts those accusations before they even reach the Father's ears. If God isn't holding those accusations against us, it's foolish for us to hold them against ourselves.

Yet, Satan's persistence, coupled with our identity crises, often leaves us wounded and feeling as though we are losing on the battlefield. It's a good thing God's truth is greater than our feelings. His promise is that if we use the weapons He's given us, we will win the battle of identity and experience the abundant life Jesus alone can give. The apostle Paul tells us the weapons God has given us to fight the enemy's attacks.

> Finally, be strong in the Lord and in his mighty power. Put on the full armor of God, so that you can take your stand against the devil's schemes. For our struggle is not against flesh and blood, but against the rulers, against the authorities, against the powers of this dark world and against the spiritual forces of evil in the heavenly realms. Therefore put on the full armor of God, so that when the day of evil comes, you may be able to stand your ground, and after you have done everything, to stand. Stand firm then, with the belt of truth buckled around your waist, with the breastplate of righteousness in place, and with your feet fitted with the readiness that comes from the gospel of peace. In addition to all this, take up the shield of faith, with which you can extinguish all the flaming arrows of the evil one. Take the helmet of salvation and the sword of the Spirit, which is the word of God. (Ephesians 6:10–17)

Paul is clear that we *will* face evil. Most likely, Paul is not referring to a specific day but is telling us we will encounter evil in our days on earth. He also uses a physical object, a Roman soldier, to illustrate a spiritual reality for those who are in Christ. Everyone in Paul's day would be familiar with the uniform worn by the typical Roman infantryman. They would have understood the importance of the armament. It existed to protect the soldier, as well as equip him to either defend the kingdom or advance it. The armor of God, spiritual in nature, functions the same in the defense and advancement of God's kingdom.

Paul actually lists the different pieces of armor in the order they would be put on in preparation for battle. He lists the belt of truth first. The belt served a couple of different purposes. First, it held the soldier's breastplate and scabbard in place. Second, it lifted and held the often long garment, or robe, worn by men of that time. People did not typically wear belts around their robes, but during times of activity, such as running or battle, they secured the garment to allow for better freedom of movement.[1] Basically, the belt helped secure the soldier within the other armor and was part of preparing for battle. Our spiritual belt of truth functions the same way. God's truth tells us that we are secure in Christ and held together by the One who will not fail. This gives us great confidence in the battle and freedom to take great steps of faith as the garment of fear and insecurity that often hinders us is securely lifted out of the way.

The breastplate was a front and back piece of armament that was typically made of bronze or chain mail.[2] Its job was to protect vital organs from the neck to the thighs. The breastplate of righteousness is no different. The righteousness given to us by God is able to guard our hearts against the lying accusations and temptations Satan throws at us. The breastplate of righteousness serves to remind us of our true positions with God.

Roman soldiers wore sandals studded with sharp nails on the bottom to increase traction and increase strength of movement.[3] Knowing that we are fitted and ready to carry the gospel of peace to the world

---

[1] *NET Bible.* Constable's notes on Ephesians 6:14.
[2] Ibid.
[3] *NET Bible.* Constable's notes on Ephesians 6:15.

gives us courage to go! We remember that Jesus Himself makes us competent as messengers of the gospel, and we are filled with an urgency to carry His message to the world.

The Roman's shield was made of wood and covered with leather. Before a battle, the leather was soaked in water so that the shield would become fireproof. This protected the soldiers from the fiery arrows that opposing armies often fired at them.[4] The soldier literally trusted his life to this shield as nothing else could save him from the arrows. The shield of faith is our trusting in God with our lives. It is trust in God for our salvation tomorrow and our deliverance today. We are able to stand our ground against the enemy's attacks because we know the One who protects us is up to the task.

The next piece of armor is the helmet. Obviously, the helmet helped protect the soldier's head from injury. The helmet of salvation serves to protect and guard our minds. It is a reminder that we are secure in our salvations. We must remember that our confidence in salvation does not come from what we can do but what Jesus has done. It's not based on who we are but on who He is. Because it's based on Him and His mighty strength, we know that it is sure. When our minds are secure in our salvations, we are better able to discern God's truth and apply it to ourselves, others, and the situations we encounter.

The final piece of armor is the sword of the Spirit, which is the Word of God. The Greek for "word" is *rhema*. Rhema does not refer to the Bible as a whole (that Greek word is *logos*) but refers to an utterance or that which was spoken. It is telling us that the sword we are to use is the scripture that is fitting for the situation. It is a word of application that tells us to call on the trump card—God's truth—to defeat the lying enemy.

---

4 Ibid.

Paul tells us it is with this armor that we are to "clothe" ourselves. It literally means to "sink into" the armor of God. We are to be immersed in this armor. It is to be applied to our lives. Here's where the rubber meets the road. The greatness of these weapons is realized through their regular applications. The weapons are applied in our lives in three ways.

1. By hearing it consistently
2. By receiving what we hear
3. By walking in obedience to what we received

So how do we do that?

James 1:19–25 tells us,

> My dear brothers and sisters, take note of this: Everyone should be quick to listen, slow to speak and slow to become angry, because human anger does not produce the righteousness that God desires. Therefore, get rid of all moral filth and the evil that is so prevalent and humbly accept the word planted in you, which can save you.
>
> Do not merely listen to the word, and so deceive yourselves. Do what it says. Anyone who listens to the word but does not do what it says is like someone who looks at his face in a mirror and, after looking at himself, goes away and immediately forgets what he looks like. But whoever looks intently into the perfect law that gives freedom, and continues in it—not forgetting what they have heard, but doing it—they will be blessed in what they do.

Verses 19 and 20 tell us we should listen way more than we should talk. James also points out how anger and bitterness in our hearts keep us from being able to honestly hear God's truth. It is hard to fully understand the gospel message and harbor bitterness and unforgiveness toward someone else. And it is impossible to look at the measure of how we have been forgiven and believe that others should not have the same.

For each of us, this points directly to our sore spots and the "they," "them," or "it" that caused them. Before you can receive God's truth, you are going to have to forgive those who've wounded you. For many of us, the person we have to forgive is ourselves. I'm not saying this is easy, but I am saying it is necessary. When you finally make the choice to forgive those who've hurt you, it removes the power they have over you.

There is a very natural progression in verses 21 through 25 as we look at the application of God's truth. We must first hear the Word of God. This does not mean that our ears hear the words as much as it means our hearts hear the message. We are then told we must receive God's Word. We cannot live out of His Word until His Word lives in us. And we must receive the message of God ourselves. Finally, we do what the Word says.

Sandwiched in between verses 22 and 25 are two very important verses. You guessed it, verses 23 and 24. In those verses, James uses an illustration that is vital to applying God's truth to our lives and utilizing the full armor of God. He tells us that listening to God's Word and then walking away and not doing what it says is like a man who looks into the mirror and then walks away and forgets what he looks like.

For most of my life I have heard those verses through a filter of condemnation. I have read those verses and heard, "Don't you dare read God's Word and then walk away, forgetting how much you don't measure up to God's standard. You aren't good enough. You never will be good enough. You don't measure up, and you never will." I bet many of you read those verses in the same degrading tone and filter of condemnation that I did. I have since realized the tone and filter I've heard those verses through was broken because of my false identity.

The truth is, when I look into God's Word, I do see how far short I come. I do see that I'm not good enough. Nor do I measure up to God's standard. I see how I *was* defined. But according to God's truth, I have a new identity! When I look into God's Word now, I realize Jesus has bridged the gap between my shortcomings and His perfection. I have been made "good enough" through Christ.

Think back to the Roman soldier in all of that armament. Think about what he saw when he looked into the mirror. He saw someone secure and ready for battle. That is what you should see when you look into God's Word. You should see

- Someone who has won the battle of identity because God's truth has trumped the lies of your experience.
- Someone who is clad and infused with the righteousness of Christ.
- Someone who is ready to carry the gospel into the world and be an eternal difference maker.
- Someone who lives with the courage that comes from knowing you have been saved, are being saved, and will be saved by the One who cannot fail.
- Someone who is able to walk through the flaming arrows of Satan's lies in a conquest to advance God's kingdom.

This is the identity God has given you, and this is what God sees. Are your eyes better or more accurate than His? No! So hear what He says, receive it, and live from it.

This is where the power of the letters we wrote come in. Those letters are infused with the truth of who we are in Christ. You need to read those letters and search the scriptures daily, as if you are looking into a mirror to remind yourself what you look like. The letter is a weapon in your arsenal to be used in the battle of identity. Hear the truth of the message that it contains, receive it, and live out of it. The truth of the message will write your better story.

Back to the story of my "beat down." The last observation we must make is that we have a God who fights for us and has never been beaten. God has never lost a battle. When we picture Jesus, many of us picture Him snuggling with a little lamb. When we think of Jesus, many of us think of Him as frail and weak. When we heard of Jesus for the first time, or as we grew up, we were often told that He is our "homeboy" or just our "friend." In our attempt to soften hearts that have been hardened by hypocritical religious Christianity, we have often misrepresented Jesus, His nature, and His character. Jesus is indeed our friend, but we must also never lose sight of the fact that He is the God of the universe and Lord.

When he saw Jesus in His post-resurrection glory, the apostle John fell on his face as though he were dead. The Bible tells us in Revelation chapter 19 that when Jesus returns for His bride, He will not be holding a lamb, barely able to get around, or wearing a shirt that says, "I am your homeboy." This is what the Bible says about Jesus's return.

> I saw heaven standing open and there before me
> was a white horse, whose rider is called Faithful
> and True. With justice he judges and wages war.

His eyes are like blazing fire, and on his head are many crowns. He has a name written on him that no one knows but he himself. He is dressed in a robe dipped in blood, and his name is the Word of God. The armies of heaven were following him, riding on white horses and dressed in fine linen, white and clean. Coming out of his mouth is a sharp sword with which to strike down the nations. "He will rule them with an iron scepter." He treads the winepress of the fury of the wrath of God Almighty. On his robe and on his thigh he has this name written:

KING OF KINGS AND LORD OF LORDS.

Whoa! That doesn't sound like a sissy King to me. That tends to shatter our childhood Sunday school image of Jesus. He is anything but weak. Jesus is a fighter, a warrior, and a brawler. He took everything Satan, the forces of hell, and the world could throw at Him and overcame it all. Jesus isn't a sissy King; He is the King of Kings who has no rival or worthy opponent. The good news is if you are in Christ, He is fighting for you and not against you. He overcame the world and gives us the ability to overcome it as well.

I want to make sure you clearly understand. I still battle every day for my identity in Christ. I still have days I feel I'm not going to make it. There are still difficult times. In fact, as I preached this message series, I could sense an increased level of attack coming from Satan. I could feel his attempts to send me back into a pit of despair. I know he wanted to take an opportunity to rob me of the life Jesus has for me. He wanted, and wants, for me to take the pen back. It's not going to happen. Now I know how to fight! I remind myself through God's Word who I am in Him on a daily basis. It's not that the pit of despair isn't there. I just have clear instructions through

God's Word that keep me from going there. I have boundaries that don't let my thought process get close to the pit any longer. And if I do slip and fall, God's Word is like a safety net that, once again, saves me and delivers me from the pit. Praise God!

CHAPTER 8

FILTER

It's pretty apparent that we live in a fast-paced society that will drive us mercilessly if we allow it. I don't know anyone who would say, "I'd love to have one more thing to do because I simply don't have enough on my plate." Most days I'm just trying to make sure the major things—like getting kids to school, not forgetting to pick them up, and making sure they eat—are covered. That means there are dozens, or even hundreds, of other details that I don't get to during the day. If you have a little obsessive-compulsive disorder in you like I do, not being on top of all the details of life can make you feel like you are going insane.

The other day I was reminded of how many details of life need my attention but don't get it when we (meaning Susan) changed the air filter in our house. Maybe you're familiar with this experience. You go to change the air filter in your home, but first you have to vacuum or wipe down the dust collected on the metal grate that holds it. When you finally get the filter out, it is so full of dust particles and dirt that you wonder how any air actually got through to the air unit. When you finally get the filter out, it is so full of dust particles and dirt that you wonder how any air actually got through to the air unit.

Somehow, even with the dirty and damaged filter, the unit manages to function, but it doesn't function to its maximum efficiency.

Because it is not functioning efficiently, it costs you money as the unit uses more electricity. Also, without proper airflow, the air does not cool as well as it could and must work harder to do what it was designed to do. I'm not trying to give you a lesson in heating and air-conditioning, but understanding how a filter works and what causes it not to work can help us win the battle of identity.

Most of us live our lives hearing information through a filter that is broken and full of condemnation and insecurity. As we've seen throughout this book, our experiences create sore spots in our lives, and those sore spots shape our identities. How we see and think of ourselves becomes the filter through which we receive all incoming data.

A broken filter leads to broken lives, even though the power of Jesus is present to heal us. If the filter through which we receive information is not God's truth, it will cost us the abundant life Jesus has promised. It will also affect the work we do for the kingdom. Even though we may work and try really hard, we will not be as productive as we would have otherwise been. When we aren't using the right filter to process information, we exhaust ourselves in a hunt for our identities rather than focus on those around us who need to find their own identities in Christ.

For example, if your experience has taught you that approval comes from doing everything perfectly and is lost if things aren't perfect, you will hear any critique, even when it is intended to be helpful, as a threat to your value and worth. Most likely you would respond with defensiveness rather than making a correction. Does that sound like you?

I see this with Christians all the time as we try to lovingly speak truth into their lives in order to help them, not hurt them. They most often become defensive and begin to play the "judgment card," saying things like, "I didn't think the church was supposed to judge people." When this happens, I realize they have misunderstood our hearts and don't understand the power of God's truth to write a better story in their lives.

A broken filter also affects the tone in which you hear God's Word. It becomes impossible to read God's Word in view of the entire Bible. For example, think about how you would read this scripture if you have spent your life striving for approval through perfectionism.

> Be perfect, therefore, as your heavenly Father is
> perfect. (Matthew 5:48)

That would be the most frustrating scripture in the Bible. You would see God as just another perfectionist taskmaster, asking you to do the undoable in order to be good enough. If experience has taught you perfection is the key to approval, reading this verse in context with the rest of scripture becomes impossible. Rather than allowing that verse to drive you to worship because Jesus did for you what you could never do on your own, it drives you to despair. You will take one of two paths. You will continue to live in despair as you constantly fall short of perfection. As a result, rather than your heart becoming more pliable and shaped like the heart of Christ, it becomes hardened by continual failure to earn what cannot be earned. The other option is that you find the burden of perfectionism too much to bear, and you simply walk away. If your filter for incoming data is perfectionism, you will either come to a place of realizing it is only through God's unmerited and unearned favor (grace) that you are able to come to Him, or you will cease to want to know Him.

Here's another scenario. Think about how a woman who lived a promiscuous life before accepting a relationship with Jesus may hear these words differently than one who did not.

Now Jesus learned that the Pharisees had heard that he was gaining and baptizing more disciples than John—although in fact it was not Jesus who baptized, but his disciples. So he left Judea and went back once more to Galilee.

Now he had to go through Samaria. So he came to a town in Samaria called Sychar, near the plot of ground Jacob had given to his son Joseph. Jacob's well was there, and Jesus, tired as he was from the journey, sat down by the well. It was about noon.

When a Samaritan woman came to draw water, Jesus said to her, "Will you give me a drink?" (His disciples had gone into the town to buy food.)

The Samaritan woman said to him, "You are a Jew and I am a Samaritan woman. How can you ask me for a drink?" (For Jews do not associate with Samaritans.)

Jesus answered her, "If you knew the gift of God and who it is that asks you for a drink, you would have asked him and he would have given you living water."

"Sir," the woman said, "you have nothing to draw with and the well is deep. Where can you get this living water? Are you greater than our father Jacob, who gave us the well and drank from it himself, as did also his sons and his livestock?"

Jesus answered, "Everyone who drinks this water will be thirsty again, but whoever drinks the water

I give them will never thirst. Indeed, the water I give them will become in them a spring of water welling up to eternal life."

The woman said to him, "Sir, give me this water so that I won't get thirsty and have to keep coming here to draw water."

He told her, "Go, call your husband and come back."

"I have no husband," she replied. Jesus said to her, "You are right when you say you have no husband. The fact is, you have had five husbands, and the man you now have is not your husband. What you have just said is quite true."

"Sir," the woman said, "I can see that you are a prophet.

The woman who has not lived promiscuously reads on and sees the goodness of God and His mercy to give new life to those who've made poor decisions. It may even correct her judgmental view of others by seeing how Jesus was willing to forgive sins and use the unlikely for His purposes. However, the other woman does not read the scripture within its context of hope. In fact, she probably doesn't finish reading the text when she is reminded that God knows her past. She never allows the truth of God's redemption to pierce her heart. Even if she does read the passage in its entirety, she struggles to view herself as the Samaritan evangelist rather than the Samaritan whore. It is the identity of the latter that becomes the filter of information as it is heard and processed. Comments that may or may not be directed at her past in any way are often heard as indictments of her former lifestyle. She connects dots to form a picture that doesn't exist in God's view of her or in the opinions of others.

Another example is if your experience with a parent or other caregiver has taught that you don't measure up to the expectations placed on you by others. Comments that have nothing to do with your performance will cause you to question your value and worth. I was actually at the Blessing Ranch the first time I recognized this in my own life. Susan and I were going through an exercise with Dr. Walker in which we were taking the lies that I believed due to my experiential truth and replacing them with scripture (the Big T) that told a different story about me. Dr. Walker asked me to turn to scriptures in my Bible that showed how God felt about me in contrast to what I believed about myself. At first my mind went blank, and I couldn't think of anything. I finally began to get my thoughts together and started pulling out scriptures that countered the lies. I left that meeting feeling like I was the biggest idiot, unspiritual, Bible-illiterate pastor on the face of the planet.

I thought about my feelings during our break, and decided to bring them up to Dr. Walker at the next session. When I explained my feelings to him, he astonished me when his reply was, "That's funny. I was thinking just the opposite. I was actually thinking that you have a very good command of the scriptures. I noticed your Bible was highlighted and underlined and thought, 'Wow, he actually reads his Bible.'"

Do you see how my broken filter heard a "truth" that wasn't even there? Because I saw myself as incompetent and not good enough, I wasn't able to correctly process the data that I was receiving. Dr. Walker gave no indication that he believed my Bible knowledge was insufficient or that I was a spiritual bozo. The data was coming through a filter that was clogged with years of lies Satan had sewn into the fabric of my mind. He sabotaged my entire thought process.

Here's the bottom line. If we are to live consistently in our new identities, we must process incoming data through the filter of God's truth, not the filter of our experience. Here's how Paul put it.

> By the humility and gentleness of Christ, I appeal to you—I, Paul, who am "timid" when face to face with you, but "bold" toward you when away! I beg you that when I come I may not have to be as bold as I expect to be toward some people who think that we live by the standards of this world. For though we live in the world, we do not wage war as the world does. The weapons we fight with are not the weapons of the world. On the contrary, they have divine power to demolish strongholds. We demolish arguments and every pretension that sets itself up against the knowledge of God, and we take captive every thought to make it obedient to Christ.

In this text, Paul is defending the ministry to which God called him. Even though the Corinthians themselves had become Christians through Paul's ministry, his credentials were still under attack. Think about that. The apostle Paul, the greatest evangelist the world has ever known, is being told that his credentials aren't as good as some other men who claimed to be apostles! Paul tells the Corinthians that when he comes to them in a future visit, he will not fight with carnal (worldly, fleshly) weapons such as manipulation, trickery, or deceit as the other men did. Rather, he will fight with spiritual weapons that are able to demolish arguments or strongholds. Earlier, we looked at how strongholds are false patterns of thinking that lead to wrong ways of living. In this case, the strongholds were arguments being made by men within the Corinthian church that negated the truth of God.

Regardless of the context of the argument that Satan so persistently proposes, exposing it to the truth of God's Word destroys it. While this attack on Paul was not directly from the hand of Satan, Satan's forces of evil directed it. Satan loves to bring accusations and arguments against us to shape the way we think and interpret the world around us. He uses experiences with people—as he attempted to do with Paul—events, and culture to formulate those arguments against us and establish wrong patterns of thinking.

As Christians, we must see the power of God's Word to squelch every argument against us before it has the opportunity to impact our thinking. Paul tells the Corinthians that any thought that is not in line with God's truth will be exposed for what it is. He is confident that every lie being told about him will be captured and taken captive by the power of God's Word. We must begin taking our thoughts captive rather than letting them take us captive!

How do we do this? We filter them through God's Word.

CHAPTER 9

STOP, THINK, PRAY

As children, three words were engrained into our minds in case we were ever somehow set on fire. To escape the flames we were told to

Stop, drop, and roll.

Okay, that's technically four words, but only three of them really matter. We were told those three words so many times that if asked, we could quote them without even thinking. Fortunately, I've never had to see if learning the words would translate into doing the words in a real emergency. I really believe if I found myself on fire, I would run around, screaming like a little girl being chased with a toad.

I'd like to introduce you to three other words that—unlike stop, drop, roll—I have had the opportunity to put into practice. I learned the application of these words at the Blessing Ranch and since then these words have been tested, and when applied, have worked. You would not want to use them to put out a physical fire, but I have seen firsthand how effective they are at putting out the flaming arrows of the enemy. Here they are.

Stop, think, pray.

I told you these wouldn't be your words of choice in a physical fire. But when used to apply God's Word, these three little words can change your life. Remembering them and putting them into practice will help you begin to redirect the information you receive through experiences, conversations, culture, and so on. Let's take a closer look at them.

Stop

Of all the signs we must obey when we drive, the stop sign may be the most important. To actually stop at a stop sign is amazingly difficult for some people to do. According to the *Urban Dictionary,* a "California stop" is, "not coming to a full stop at a stop sign or running it all together." Our resistance to actually slowing down to a complete stop is a symptom of our breakneck pace in life. Let's be honest; slowing down is a hassle. Actually stopping is unthinkable.

If we are going to win the battle of identity, we must learn to stop and intercept information that is coming in from outside influences. We typically run through the day so fast that we just depend on our autoprogramming to get us through. I have found that being rushed causes us to be more distracted. The more distracted we are, the more we depend on habit to get us through the day.

The problem with allowing habit to get us through the day is that we've all developed bad habits, especially in regard to how we think and process information. In regards to the battle for our identity, stop is actually taking a moment to get out of autopilot and intercept incoming information. With thousands of experiences, conversations, and encounters each day, it is impossible to intercept every piece of data that you receive. So just start by being conscious of those influences that really push on your sore spot. Those things that tend to cause you to fall into the pit of despair, provoke you to anger, and so on. Our goal is to heal the sore spots and create new filters through our new identities.

I imagine most of us have had the miserable experience of getting a sunburn. It seems that no one wants to pat you on the back until it is burned from forgetting to reapply your sunscreen. If someone starts to pat you on the back, you instantly turn away from the person or try to block his or her hand. Why? Because your back is sore, and you don't want the person's big paw hitting it! Once the sunburn is healed, people can pat all they want to (not really, that would be weird) because it no longer hurts.

Healing the sore spot caused by our experiences is very similar. If we stop and intercept the incoming influences that push on our sore spots, they will have the opportunity to heal. Remember, we are renewing our minds through God's truth. It is a process. Let's start with those things that, if intersected, can allow the sore spot to heal.

As we stop, we move from autopilot to actually taking control of what information and small "T" truths we allow into our minds and hearts.

Think

Think is the process of bringing incoming information to the truth of Christ. We stop the information and then we analyze the information through God's truth. This is when the letter you wrote earlier is really able to be powerful. This is also why memorizing scripture and being in God's Word consistently are so important. There is no other option but to accept the truth of our experiences if we don't have the Word of God in us to speak a greater truth. We cannot live out of God's Word until God's Word lives in us!

Thinking is where we pull out the sword of the Spirit, the Word of God, to defeat the enemy's lies. We take that part of God's truth that is applicable to the moment and lay it over the lie. We see the lie for what it is, and God's truth trumps what our experiences would have otherwise told us.

The apostle Paul gives us this instruction.

> Finally, brothers and sisters, whatever is true, whatever is noble, whatever is right, whatever is pure, whatever is lovely, whatever is admirable— if anything is excellent or praiseworthy—*think* about such things. Whatever you have learned or received or heard from me, or seen in me—put it into practice. And the God of peace will be with you (emphasis mine).

When we allow God's truth to dictate our patterns of thinking, we overcome the destructive patterns we have learned. Paul tells them that whatever they have "learned" from him should be put into practice. What Paul taught them was the truth! Knowing the truth will set us free as it becomes our filter of information. Practicing the truth always leads us to a better story!

As we think, we begin to replace the message we would normally hear through our broken filter with God's message.

Pray

Praying is bringing the incoming data and our hearts before God. When we do this, we allow God to show us how our hearts line up with what we are receiving as well as His truth. With all incoming data, there are only two responses that we are able to make, application and interception.

Application happens when we intersect the incoming data (stop), bring it into the truth of Christ (think), bring it before God (pray), and realize the information is true. Second Timothy 3:16 and 17 says,

> All Scripture is God-breathed and is useful for teaching, rebuking, correcting and training in righteousness, so that the servant of God may be thoroughly equipped for every good work.

When we read God's Word and bring our experiential truth to God's Word, we often find that we are out of line with God's truth and will for us. We all need to be taught, rebuked, corrected, and trained by God's inspired Word. We are not always right! Living without condemnation does not mean that we live without needing to be taught, rebuked, corrected, or trained. But notice that Paul tells Timothy teaching, rebuking, correcting, and training all come from God's Word, not from our experiences. The Bible is our teacher, not our experiences. It is vital that we interpret our experiences through the filter of scripture and not interpret scripture through the filter of experience.

It is also important to realize teaching, rebuking, correcting, and training are able to take place without condemnation. If we are in Christ, God is our Corrector as a loving Father, not our condemner as a begrudging tyrant! Even as an imperfect father, I never discipline my children to hurt them. How unloving of me is it if I allow my two-year-old to run through the parking lot without correcting him. While he may not like it at the moment, it is much more loving and better for him if I correct his destructive behavior. Once we see that through Jesus we are children of a loving Father, we are able to receive teaching, correcting, training, and even rebuking without condemnation. Why? We now understand God's teaching and discipline are about us being brought back into and staying in God's will for our life, not our value and worth to God.

Interception happens when we intersect the incoming data (stop), bring it into the truth of Christ (think), bring it before God (pray) and realize the information to be false. Interception is allowing God's truth to step in front of the incoming data in order to keep it from being received into our minds and hearts. The only place for this data to be filed is in the trash. Get rid of it! It stinks, is spoiled, and can be of no use to you or anyone else.

I imagine most of us have had the experience of using a computer to print a document. When a computer is set up, it is typically set up with a "default" printer. This is the printer that is automatically used by the computer unless settings are changed or overridden. This is very similar to the way we process information as it comes in from the world around us. We have a default filter that processes the data and tells us how we should interpret it. Unfortunately, our interpretations are often not consistent with reality or the truth of God's Word. The goal is to create a new default filter. What this means is that every bit of information we receive during the day—whether a TV ad, constructive criticism, mean-spirited criticism, or pressure from the expectations of others—is routed through God's truth before it is allowed to impact our minds and hearts. Until we override our old settings through the power of God's truth, the lies of Satan will be printed on our minds and hearts rather than the story God desires to write in their place.

Practicing stop, think, pray begins to rewire our minds. We no longer default to analyzing data that comes to us through the things we've learned from our experiences. Stop, think, pray begins to allow God's Word to be the filter through which we process information about others, the world, and ourselves. Practicing this consistently may seem impossible at first. But with time and consistent application, you will be surprised how natural this process becomes.

When I first started redirecting data through God's truth by practicing stop, think, pray, I was amazed by the number of thoughts I had in a day that were simply lies. My first thought was, *No wonder I'm exhausted!* My mind was constantly analyzing every piece of incoming information for a clue to my true identity.

When I was a boy, my dad got interested in finding Civil War relics. He got a metal detector, and we went on walks through the woods of west Georgia, waving that metal detector over the ground in search of a bullet, knife, musket, or other artifact. It was cool to find something that was over a hundred years old. But it was also exhausting as you scoured the countryside, walking and digging in search of hidden treasure.

The way I searched for nuggets of treasure reminds me of how, when we aren't secure in our identities in Christ, we scour every conversation, commercial, and encounter for clues as to who we are. It is exhausting, and it takes our eyes off of Jesus and others and puts them on us. The problem is we will never find identity, healing, or fulfill our God-given purpose by looking at ourselves. If we could heal ourselves, we would have done it a long time ago! Healing only comes by keeping our eyes and hearts fixed on Christ.

By learning to stop, think, pray, we are able to destroy old strongholds in our minds and create a healthy filter for receiving the data bombarding us from the world. When we do this, our sore spots are able to heal, and we begin the process of becoming whole. While stop, think, pray takes some work, the fruit of our labor will be worth it.

Be encouraged that we don't have to live in bondage to a false identity or the condemnation that comes with it. We can truly experience what it is to be free in Christ. Stop, think, pray and the truth will set you free!

CONCLUSION

I will not tell you that the battle is gone because it still exists. However, today it is different because I know how to hit the pitches Satan throws at me. I'm not perfect at dealing with the Little T truth that experience tries to throw at me ... but I am better at it.

Since I wrote the original manuscript for this book, two and a half years have passed. Our church has more than doubled in size, we have planted two other campuses in communities in our area, we tripled our staffing, brought on ten to fifteen interns, and seen hundreds more salvations and baptisms. The point of telling you about all these things is not to brag or pat myself on the back. The point is to show you that my circumstances and the pressures surrounding them have not changed. There is more pressure and more going on now than there has ever been. But while the circumstances in my life have not changed, I have. I can't tell you that the circumstances you are in are going to get better, but I can tell you that you can get better at dealing with your circumstances. It all starts with growing into a healthy identity.

Now for me, incoming information must line up with the identity I already have in Christ before it is granted access into my mind and heart. My identity is held securely by Jesus rather than being held captive by the world. The great news is that this isn't just the story God wants to write in my life, He wants this for you as well. If you are in Christ, the truth will set you free. That promise is true today. Let God's truth be the filter of information. Let the helmet of salvation protect your mind from the lies of Satan. Allow the breastplate of righteousness to shield your heart from condemnation. Wield the sword of the Spirit, God's Word, and defeat the enemy of fallen experience. Stand secure in God's truth, and don't be moved by every wave of criticism that comes along. Live confidently behind the shield of faith that extinguishes every fiery arrow Satan has designed to wound your soul. And run as a herald of the greatest news that has ever rang through the ears of fallen humanity and pierced the hearts of billions: the Gospel. Go and tell the world that there is a better story. Go and tell the world God's story.

I hope this book will set you on a path toward a healthy identity and the freedom Jesus died for us to have. Practicing the principles that I learned at The Blessing Ranch and that are outlined here has truly transformed my life and brought me so much further into the freedom I know Jesus wants for me. He will do the same for you.